PLATFORMS
OF
SUCCESS

*What the New Generation of Elite Sellers Are Doing
and How it Can Work for You*

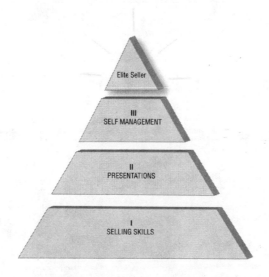

By
Scott Johnson

PLATFORMS OF SUCCESS

by Scott Johnson

Edited by Julia F. Freeman

Charts and Illustrations by China Fleck

authorHOUSE®

AuthorHouse™
1663 Liberty Drive
Bloomington, IN 47403
www.authorhouse.com
Phone: 1-800-839-8640

Edited by: Julia F. Freeman
Charts and Illustrations by: China Fleck

© 2009 J. Scott Johnson. All rights reserved.

No part of this book may be reproduced, stored in a retrieval system, or transmitted by any means without the written permission of the author.

First published by AuthorHouse 4/1/2009

ISBN: 978-1-4389-7365-4 (sc)
ISBN: 978-1-4389-7384-5 (hc)
ISBN: 978-1-4389-7385-2 (e)

Library of Congress Control Number: 2009903614

Printed in the United States of America
Bloomington, Indiana

This book is printed on acid-free paper.

In memoriam

Tom C. Johnson
(1922-2005)

This book would not have been written if not for three people:

my dearest mother who taught me how to write it,
my wife who inspired me to finish it,
and my son who someday may write his own.

TABLE OF CONTENTS

PROLOGUE
Knowing is not enough; we must apply. Willing is not enough; we must do...Goethe (1749-1832)

Before I became a manager of sellers, I was a seller. And before I became a seller, I was a teacher of sellers. That I not only preached, but was forced to practice my preachings, makes all the difference in what you can learn from this book.

Source and Inspiration
You see, I not only took every "train the trainer" type program I could find, during my own seminars, I videotaped and catalogued hundreds of role-plays from thousands of students. Then, I took both what I taught and what I learned and applied it in my real life selling situations, refining as I went. When recruited to hire, train, and motivate a sales force across 15 states, I often accompanied team members on their sales calls, taking notes, providing what I hoped was constructive critiques and then filing away what I (we) learned for the day when I might write this book.

I taught at least one such sales course (each lasting three days) each month for over ten years until, eventually, I formed my own speaking and consulting company, JSJ Learning Systems, Inc. I gave keynote or sales and time management presentations to associations, businesses, and conventions around the US and became an enthusiastic member of both the National and Florida Speakers Associations. Along the way, I continued expanding my repertoire of "what worked" and "what didn't work," blending my personal skills catalogue with relevant scientific studies on persuasion and the psychology of buying and selling, again, in anticipation of the day when I might write this book.

Group Presentations

Later, I was drafted into service for a small software company and given the title vice president of Sales & Marketing. As such, my primary directive was to gain the endorsement of a computerized insurance policy rating system by giving sales presentations to boards of directors of state associations of insurance agents. I was also charged to make similar presentations to the top executives of America's largest insurance carriers.

I used the techniques from my seminars to present the functions of the system—the price, the service contract, the required hardware and the monthly download fee—complimented by an automated projection system so arcane it would have today's PowerPoint enthusiast rolling in the aisles. I presented twice a day: once in the morning, then once in the afternoon usually after driving to another city. In each case, after asking for a deposit check to "lock in today's price," it was on to the next city, day after every weekday until Fridays when, exhausted, we dragged our bags, computers, projectors, and ourselves to the nearest airport for the plane ride back home. I closed thousands of individual sales and the total number of large group presentations in my career, to date, easily numbers several hundred.

Self Management

But, I wasn't only refining skills and cataloguing group and face-to-face selling situations; I was developing a system for establishing and reaching goals, both personal and business-related. I was learning the importance of planning. I was learning how to manage myself and my time so I could spend what time was left doing the things I enjoyed.

Of course, I also had to manage the time of those who worked for me, some more than others. Together we worked on ways to make ourselves more productive—ways to eliminate time wasters so we could spend more time selling.

At one point, as part of an overall quest for better self management, my entire sales team conducted an internal time audit. All the sellers (myself included) and administrative staff members began keeping logs of how we spent our time. A cadre of sellers working in fifteen other states faxed their reports to me at the close of each business day, which for purposes of our experiment began at 7:00 a.m.

These time logs and the teachings of time management experts like Dr. John Lee, then a professor at Florida State University, provided much of the foundation for my speaking business and the development of the self and time management "proficiencies" in Platform III of this book. I believe they can help anyone, particularly motivated sellers, achieve meaningful goals.

Platforms of Success

Over a period just shy of two decades, I became convinced there were three platforms to Elite Status and a successful career in selling, as follows: Platform I—proficiency in face-to-face selling situations; Platform II—skill presenting or selling to groups, large and small; and, Platform III—the ability to manage yourself and your time for maximum impact.

I've used the term "Platform" because proficiency at one level is necessary to advance and develop proficiency at the next level. This is sometimes the forgotten part of achieving success in today's brave new world of selling. A seller who is organized, punctual, and disciplined may be quite capable at managing his/her time and thus has many appointments with qualified prospects. But what good are appointments when, due to lack of proficiency from Platform I, sales aren't closed? Likewise, with group presentations. You may be very, very good on your feet, in a boardroom, or in front of a large audience. But, inducing members of a "group" to part with their money and commit to buy your product or service requires skills acquired in Platform I and then modified to fit the unique characteristics of a group environment in Platform II.

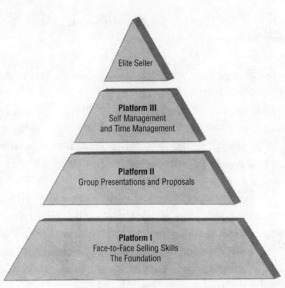

PLATFORMS OF SUCCESS

You'll find the information in this book clustered accordingly: Platform I deals with the skills necessary to manage the traditional over the desk sales call; Platform II covers the application of those same techniques to a corporate board room or large convention as I had done; and, Platform III is about how Elite Sellers, indeed any ambitious executive, can manage time more effectively to establish and meet personal and professional goals. In Platform I there are two general subject areas—one pertains to the skills themselves; the other can be called "The Foundation" because logically it comes first and secondarily it also underpins the skills in Platform II.

However, in all three Platforms, indeed throughout, I try to avoid just talking theory or spending too much time motivating you to succeed or work harder (smarter perhaps). I figure you're motivated enough already or you wouldn't be reading this book. I also figure either your employer or the financial or emotional rewards of success will provide ample motivation. Fact is, once you develop a modicum of proficiency at the skills in this book, you'll find at least some motivation from their application and efficacy.

That's why *Platforms of Success* places greater emphasis on empirical examples of the skill or concept being taught and how to adapt it to your unique sales environment. Whenever possible, appropriate phrases or samples of statements illustrating the skills are included and are adapted from actual sales calls and student role-plays. Charts, graphs, and other tools appear where beneficial as well as recaps or important summaries when helpful. The Appendix highlights some of the lessons or skills under the title "snap shots" and contains other items referenced in preceding chapters.

As in my seminars, the emphasis is on building habits, new habits—habits that can propel serious goal oriented individuals through each Platform and ultimately into Elite Status as a seller of any product. Master the skills and techniques within each platform and you'll find immense reward, both financially and emotionally; you'll also experience the satisfaction of knowing you've reached the status of an Elite Seller...I promise.

PLATFORM I

The Foundation

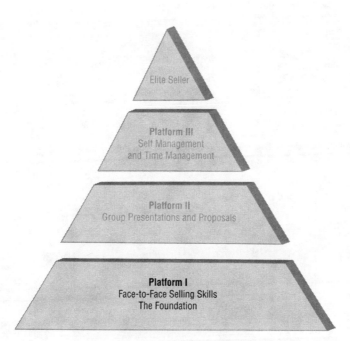

PLATFORMS OF SUCCESS

1

Chapter 1

THE SELLER'S EVOLUTION
Everyone lives by selling something...Robert Louis Stevenson

When I first began studying and categorizing skills of the sellers I considered to be "Elite," it was the middle 1970s when sales training, generally, had begun its transformation. Corporate America, it appeared, was turning away from a singular focus that stressed working harder or that tied success to more calls and more appointments, and was moving instead to something more interpersonal and instructive, something better.

Before the 70s, early training programs were obsessed with motivation, merely urging new sales recruits to not be afraid to cold call and, always, always...ask for the order. In the 50s and 60s trainees were being told to never be timid, never be intimidated, and never take "No!" for an answer. While modern clinical psychology and Peter Drucker may have assigned other motivations, it appeared to me it was simply easier to push new recruits to work harder than it was to train them to work smarter.

That was the 70s metamorphosis. Today's world is different still; the Internet and technology have seen to that. In 1978, a skit on the hit television show *Saturday Night Live (SNL)* illustrated the difference. Set in a boutique that specialized in Scotch tape, the owners were totally miffed at not having any customers. How could this be when "...we have so many varieties of scotch tape?" Back then... hilarious!

Today, *SNL's* skit wouldn't make any sense. Today, gen-x-ers and the millennials (born between 1980 and 1995) shop at stores that sell only yogurt or rice pudding or home furnishings in a single color. Today, there are 19,000 variations of Starbucks coffee and 26,893 new food and household products introduced, including: 115 deodorants, 187 breakfast cereals, and 303 women's fragrances. And, to get someone to buy...nobody had to knock on a door, get a signature on a check, make a presentation...or refuse to take "No!" for an answer!

Technology and a "trillion" choices changed corporate America and, in doing so, changed corporate Americans. The Internet delivers anything to anybody, leaving most sellers taking orders on the phone, or worse, just processing orders on a computer. Our economic world is largely commoditized and it's getting more so every day.

On the other hand, today's Elite Sellers (and tomorrow's millennials) are more specialized and far more valuable...and also becoming more so everyday. They sell, or will sell, the products that help others sell the commodities—the high-end intangibles like financial services, information technologies, integrated software and hardware systems, securities, commercial insurance, investment properties, virtual technology, IPOs, and venture capital.

Those who sell successfully in today's (and tomorrow's) new economy, the Elite, while they are consummate technicians in their industries, they also recognize the customer is king and won't buy anything merely because a seller was the last to ask or the one who asked more than anyone else.

A seller using Elite Skills is trusted more by buyers because he/she understands that people buy because a product or service satisfies their needs. The Elite Seller of today's high-end intangible isn't the loudest voice in the room, but is the one most often heard. Price and service matter, of course, but with high-end intangibles customers also buy because the seller satisfied their need to be heard and to be understood in an increasingly impersonal, commoditized world.

Chapter 2

BUYERS & SELLERS

If one tells the truth, one is sure, sooner or later, to be found out...
Oscar Wilde.

It may be important to some to understand the nomenclature used in this book, particularly the meanings of the words "Buyers & Sellers."

In the context of Elite Selling, there are only three kinds of people: those who buy; those who sell; and, those who do both. I make this distinction, recognizing that you are reading this book, this section, this paragraph, this sentence, because you (or maybe someone you know) are involved in selling as a career. That makes you (or the someone you know) a seller, even if you aren't successful. Even if no one ever buys from you; you are a seller because you engage in activities intended to cause someone else to buy.

Those you sell to are buyers, even if they don't buy anything from you. They are in the role of a buyer and, ultimately, they will buy, perhaps just not from you, or not "today," or perhaps not even the product that you claim will solve all their problems.

There are other reasons to refer to someone who sells as a seller instead of an account executive or a marketing rep—names designed to distract from the traditional connotation. Seller refers to an action, not a position or a title. A person who sells is a seller; an "account" executive, or marketer is intended to imply something more—perhaps, customer management, advertising, deal making, or a host of other activities. Another term, producer, means something else still. A producer can produce a lot of things and do it in a lot of ways. A producer can simply take orders for products people "must" buy. Producers of recurring products, like insurance, can rely on the three "Rs" (renewals, referrals, and relatives) to produce revenue.

But, for purposes of this book, a seller is someone who must convince someone else to buy their product when that someone else (the buyer) may not have otherwise been inclined to do so.

This is why I say if you want to do something other than sell, or if you fancy yourself "more" than just a seller, then you need something other than, or more than, just this book. Platforms of Success is about selling and people who engage in selling. It's about what is done and said when someone is face-to-face with a buyer or a group of potential buyers. It's about how you analyze what a buyer is saying and how you go about convincing buyers to "buy" your product and to buy it from you. And, it's about how you can manage your time and yourself to do these things better and more often.

Again, there are many steps in the sales process—canvassing, prospecting, cold calling, getting appointments, gathering information...all important and, in fact, usually indispensable. Each step, however, while often requiring or rewarding other talents or knowledge, will never substitute for face-to-face skill and training.

So I say, keep in mind you are a seller. Be good at it. Be proud of it. Tell others that's what you do and tell them you are good at it! They will not only respect your candor, but on the day they need an honest opinion about your product or service, instead of calling an account executive with your competitor...they'll likely call you instead.

Chapter 3

HABIT & PRACTICE
If you can't ask someone to buy when you think they don't want to buy, put down this book and change professions...sj

Instead of *Platforms of Success*, a better title might have been "Everything I've Learned That I Think You Should Know About." I say this because in the earliest days of my career I was mostly discovering what worked, what didn't work, and what was most likely to avoid failure. The truth is, in looking back, I'm able to know I could've been more successful at selling (as one example), if all I did was avoid a few selling mistakes. I didn't have to be the "slickest" seller on the block; I could meet minimum success levels by simply avoiding big errors.

A Matter of Habit
Selling, like much of your personality, is largely a matter of habit—habits formed by a background and a life experience uniquely your own, and habits formed in part because of your genetic makeup. The two, experience and genetics, make you what you are and, taken together, are why you do and say the things you do and say during a sales call.

Achieving Elite Status is about changing those habits. Platform I examines the sales call, defines and categorizes buyer comments, and then teaches the structure of the perfect response. The names for the categories of buyer comments are logical. Frankly, you'll learn the name or category of every possible buyer comment. But, nomenclature isn't the secret to success. You can change the names if you want. What's important is that you recognize the buyer's comment and know the appropriate response and be able to deliver it at the appropriate time in the appropriate way.

But, the truth is, most of what succeeds has been explored, dissected, explained, and practiced by thousands of successful, and yes, unsuccessful sellers. Besides, what's difficult about selling isn't knowing (or not knowing) what to do and say during a sales call. Rather, it's doing and saying it once you know.

Like the buyer comments, the seller's responses are also imminently logical and based, in many cases, on surveys or scientific analysis I gleaned from other sources. As it is, however, just recognizing and agreeing with the rationale for a particular sales statement is the easy part. Building the habit of giving that response, consistently, without hesitation, is the key. And, it only takes one thing…practice!

Yes, good old-fashioned practice will make you a better seller. Once you learn the techniques of Elite Sellers, you can practice on buyers, on friends or in role-plays with co-workers, your sales manager, or your bathroom mirror. The important thing is that you recognize now, before you go any further in your sales career, that selling is about developing habits. If you can't change those habits, the habits of what you say; if you can't close a sale when it's "technically" time to do so simply because you feel uncomfortable doing it; if you can't keep yourself from talking when it's "technically" time to listen, then do yourself a favor—stop reading this book and get into another profession. You will never enjoy selling. You may make a living at it, depending on the product you sell and its competitiveness, but I guarantee it will be in spite of, and not because of, your ability or talent as a seller.

On the other hand, if you're serious about changing some habits and achieving Elite Status as a seller, keep reading.

Chapter 4

A SELLER'S PERSONALITY

*Those with high empathy have few enemies and can be well
liked by buyers. Unfortunately, their sales figures never
quite measure up...sj*

Everyone has a unique selling personality. In my early days administering a course developed by Xerox Learning Systems, I taught that a seller's personality was divided into three different parts: Drive, (sometimes called, Ego Drive), Empathy, and Intelligence. This came to me from Dr. Herb Greenberg, founder of the Caliper Corporation, which counsels corporations on hiring effective (Elite) sellers. I not only required all my students to complete Caliper's survey and assessment, I took it myself to learn how my Drive, Empathy, and Intelligence would help me become an Elite Seller.

Drive
This is the inner need to persuade others. Drive, in this context, doesn't have anything to do with making money except that more money from selling often means you've persuaded others successfully. A sales person with high Drive wants and needs the victory, the successful persuasion, as a powerful enhancement of ego. Self-esteem is enhanced by such a victory and diminished when failing to persuade. Usually, someone with hefty Drive is not discouraged by failure. In fact, they are often even more challenged by it. The

driven individual wants and needs to persuade not primarily for the practical benefits or material gains (money, promotion, or other rewards), but more importantly for the feeling of satisfaction that comes from the victory. *Successful persuasion, then, is the particular means through which the Ego Driven individual gains pleasure and ego-gratification* —Greenberg.

Empathy

Empathy should not be confused with sympathy. Highly sympathetic people are rarely good sellers. They fret about making people do something they perceive they do not want to do. The hardest thing for someone with too much sympathy to do is to sell something they would not buy.

Empathy, on the other hand, is an extremely valuable sales tool. It is the capacity to recognize the clues and cues provided by others in order to relate effectively to them. Sympathetic people over identify with others and often lose site of the objective. The Empathetic individual is objectively and accurately able to identify the feelings of others without necessarily agreeing with them. This ability allows someone to gain powerful feedback from others and, according to Greenberg, to *adjust their own behavior in order to deal effectively with a buyer or client.*

Intelligence

Simply put, Intelligence is the ability to apply knowledge you have and to quickly acquire knowledge you don't have. Intelligence matters no matter what you do. Depending on the product you sell, it might be a big advantage to have a high IQ, particularly if those you sell to or the product you sell requires it. In Elite Selling, however, you need only have enough intelligence to learn some common sense techniques. If you've read this far, you have the minimum amount of Intelligence necessary to acquire the secrets of Elite Sellers. It's the application of those techniques through practice and experience that distinguishes the successful seller from one who merely has a high IQ. Because they reflect the actions of those who have superior intellects, having command of the skills of the Elite Seller will make anyone seem more intelligent and help them experience success levels equivalent to sellers with higher IQs.

The Elite Mix

An Elite Seller's "selling" personality always reflects a favorable ratio of Drive to Empathy; or at least his/her responses and comments do. Without proper training in Elite Selling techniques a highly driven person is often too pushy, occasionally turning buyers off or getting into arguments with them. A high Ego Driven seller often attempts to close the sale too early or too often, never picking up on buyer cues that tell a more Empathetic Elite Seller it's not time to close or which type of close to use.

Conversely, those with too much Empathy are usually not good closers. They are often convinced the buyer isn't ready to buy, or is reluctant or wants to wait, and...rather than find out for sure, by closing, they simply fail to ask for the order at all. Ego Driven individuals may make a few enemies here and there. Those with high Empathy have very few enemies and can be well liked by buyers. Unfortunately, their sales figures never quite measure up.

An Elite Seller has the perfect ratio of Ego Drive to Empathy. An Elite Seller rarely wishes he/she hadn't said something during a sales call because the Elite Seller speaks based on cues from the customer instead of features of the product—more on what the customer needs to hear than what the seller wants to talk about. Responses to customer statements made by Elite

Sellers have a "structure" that reflects the perfect mix of Empathy and Ego Drive. These statements often employ words first spoken by the buyer and mentally recorded by the seller for use later in the call.

Finally, the Elite Seller either makes the sale (achieving the desired objective for the call) or learns early on that the sale or objective is unobtainable and, therefore, departs the premises sooner rather than later.

Chapter 5

"THE" SECRET

The most important thing in communication is to hear what isn't being said...Peter Drucker

Selling at the Elite level is based on one basic principle—the principle that most people do things and buy things based on their needs.

A need could be anything, really. It could be the need to operate a business more profitably or the need to be recognized favorably by others or the need to save money or the need to provide an income for a family...or all or none of these.

The underlying goal of the Elite Selling process is uncovering buyer needs. To sell anything, you must satisfy at least the minimum needs necessary to convince a buyer to part with his or her money. But, the difficult thing isn't in knowing how to satisfy a buyer need; it's in finding out what those needs are in the first place.

Let me illustrate by retelling a story that first made the rounds after World War II.

> There's a train on its way from Paris to Madrid. In one compartment are four people: a young, beautiful girl traveling with her

elderly grandmother, and an old, stately general accompanied by a young, handsome second lieutenant. The foursome sits quietly as the train enters a tunnel.

It's pitch-black in the tunnel when suddenly the sound of a kiss is heard followed by the sound of a face being slapped. When the train pulls out of the tunnel, the four passengers, embarrassed by what they thought happened, sit silently without acknowledging the incident.

The young girl thinks to herself: "Gosh, I sure enjoyed that wonderful kiss from the handsome lieutenant. But, my grandmother slapped him so hard he'll probably not do it again in the next tunnel."

The grandmother thinks to herself: "Why, that fresh young man! He kissed my granddaughter. But, I raised her properly and she responded by giving him a good smack! I'm proud of her and know that young man will keep his hands off of her in the next tunnel."

The general thinks to himself: "I can't get over it. My aide went to West Point and I personally handpicked him. With all his training, he should have known better than to kiss that young girl. But, in the dark, she obviously thought it was me and I'm the one who got slapped. When we get back to base I'm going to give him what for!"

The young lieutenant thinks to himself: "Man that was awesome! How often do you get to kiss a beautiful young girl and slap your boss at the same time?"

The point is people rarely interpret events the same way. It all depends on your unique perspective, needs, problems, or life experiences. What the seller may think is the primary feature or selling point of a product doesn't matter. It's what the buyer thinks is important that matters. Find that out and you've uncovered the key to successfully closing the sale. Don't find it out and closing the sale is infinitely more difficult.

Benefit-Based Selling

For those who have taken sales training programs or who are selling veterans, I ask that you avoid the tendency to skip what may appear like just another explanation of Features and Benefits. Review your understanding of the concepts and learn them in the context of Elite Sellers by reading this chapter to its end. Now, let's start at the beginning.

It doesn't matter what sales course you take. It will begin (or should) by emphasizing the difference between features and benefits.

So, what's a feature? A feature is simply a characteristic of your product or service usually expressed in a word or a phrase. Out of context it has no value to your client or buyer. It only takes on value when it satisfies a need, problem, or concern of your buyer. A windshield wiper is a feature of most automobiles. A deductible is a feature of most automobile insurance policies.

What's a benefit? A benefit is the satisfaction of a buyer need provided by a feature of your product or service. The feature of a windshield wiper yields the benefit of being able to see in inclement weather. It may make driving a bit safer when it rains. The feature of an insurance policy deductible can be a benefit to a cost conscious buyer by substantially lowering the price of the policy.

What sometimes becomes difficult, and what is important in mastering the techniques of Elite Selling, is recognizing that different buyers may have different needs satisfied by the same product feature. A buyer in Seattle, which has extremely high annual rainfall, may experience a greater or different benefit from windshield wipers than someone who drives mostly in Phoenix where it practically never rains.

Also, you must learn that it is extremely important to allow the buyer to express their needs first, before you tell them about the feature that will solve their needs. Your job as an Elite Seller is to uncover buyer needs and satisfy them with the right benefit of your product or service. It is not your job to merely list or explain the features "you" think are important, state the price, and ask for the order.

Listening and Questioning

If I had to pick the one thing that I think would make more people successful at selling over any other single thing, it wouldn't be a lower price or a faster delivery date. It wouldn't be more buyers or better packaging. It wouldn't be a brighter smile or a new suit of clothes. It would simply be to become a better listener.

Of the hundreds of role-plays I've observed and critiqued in my career, and of all the sales calls I've made or accompanied others on, the most common flaw is that of talking too much and listening too little. The only way someone can know what's on a buyer's mind is if the buyer says what's on his/her mind, and they can't do that if you're doing all the talking. Most (and I do mean most) salespeople talk, and talk, and talk.

Both as a manager of sellers and as a seller, I've seen it happen dozens of times: the sale was made, the buyer was ready (even eager) to buy, but…the seller wasn't through selling. The seller was so busy talking about all the wonderful features that they knew so much about, that they never heard what the buyer was "trying" to say. And even if they did, it didn't matter…*they* still had more they wanted to say and by God they were going to say it no matter what trivial needs the buyer may have been trying to express.

Occasionally, even after closing the sale, I've heard the seller keep on talking so much that they wound up creating objections the buyer was never concerned about in the first place and, eventually, they lost the sale.

Motivational Listening

Besides, listening has benefits beyond just providing sellers with information about the buyer's needs. Listening in and of itself helps close the sale. It's motivational. People like someone who listens. It makes them feel good. Buyers like to talk and they like to be listened to.

That you learn what needs a buyer has when you listen is, of course, very important. That you develop a connection with a buyer and make them feel good about you, your product, or service, is also important. After all, the whole idea is to make it easy for a buyer to "sign on the dotted line." That's hard for "any" buyer to do with someone they don't know, have a problem communicating with, or, worst of all, don't trust.

Having someone listen to you when you speak, learn from what you say, and respond according to what they learned is motivational. It builds rapport. Rapport builds trust. Trust increases the chances of the buyer saying "yes." Listening is, therefore, the number one secret, indeed the foundation, for becoming an Elite Seller.

I recall a story of a grand European cathedral that was disassembled brick by brick, placed in pieces on an ocean liner, then transported and reassembled in the US. I believe it's helpful for sellers to think of listening in this context. Every conversation with a buyer is an ex-

LISTENING IS AT THE CENTER OF ELITE SELLING

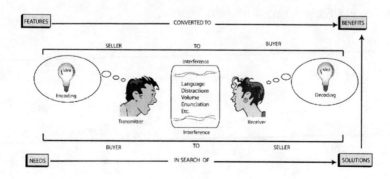

change of ideas. Each person in a conversation has or develops "ideas" that must be disassembled and then transmitted to a listener who must reassemble or "decode" the message in order to have the same mental concept that existed in the mind of the transmitter. Interference with this process comes in all shapes and sizes. In selling, it would be good if the interference is never from the failure of the seller to listen, truly listen, to what the customer is saying.

The question has always been "Okay, I need to listen, but…what if the buyer isn't talking or what if they aren't saying anything relevant to the sales call?" Good Question!! That's why the second most important overriding aspect of successful selling, the second best secret of the Elite Seller, is questioning. Yes, you've got to be both a skilled questioner and a talented listener to maximize your number of successful closings. The two go hand in glove. And, when they fit just right, it's time to close the sale.

So there you have it. The secret(s) of the Elite Seller summed up in just three basic skills: 1.) Questioning to get buyers to talk; 2.) Listening and responding appropriately when they do, and; 3.) Closing the sale.

But…remember I said that there really aren't any new secrets to selling and that reaching Elite Status is more about developing habits than it is about learning secrets?

It's true.

So, now let's look in more detail at these three skills and examine some ways to begin building new habits.

PLATFORM I

Selling Skills

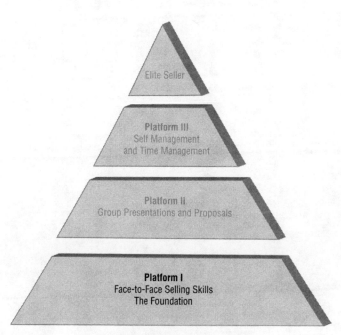

Elite Seller

Platform III
Self Management
and Time Management

Platform II
Group Presentations and Proposals

Platform I
Face-to-Face Selling Skills
The Foundation

PLATFORMS OF SUCCESS

Chapter 6

GETTING AROUND THE BASES
Spending less time in front of a buyer who isn't going to buy is just as important as spending more time in front of one who might...sj

In the Prologue I mentioned that, for one stretch in my career lasting almost ten years, I taught at least one, sometimes two, sales seminars a month. They were small, intense groups of never more than twelve individuals; eight was the optimum number.

We spent the better part of three days and one evening, using every tool I could muster to help young or inexperienced sellers build new and better habits. In the mornings we learned the skills you are going to read about in this Platform and in the afternoon the students videotaped each other "role-playing" the skills they learned in the morning.

The videos worked miracles. It's one thing to role-play in front of a small audience. It's another to do it on camera! And, when the peer group critique of your selling skills can be verified by reviewing the video, it's a powerful tool for building new habits.

The RASSCL Principles
About the same time, I began to research the science of persuasion

and the psychology that drives buyers to make decisions or to react to statements from sellers. While there is a lot of information available on this subject the most respected and usable source in my opinion is the world's most quoted expert on social persuasion, Regents Professor of Psychology and Marketing Robert Cialdini at Arizona State University. Prior to writing this book, I combined my empirical observations (both on-site selling and in the classroom) with Cialdini's science-based principles (and the skills from XLS) to create both the structure for an entire sales call and the steps for various skills used in a sales call. Cialdini's research reveals six universal principles that influence buying decisions. These principles (I use the acronym RASSCL), while occasionally referenced, were always considered in designing the skills in Platform I and II. As you read, if you look close enough, you'll find adherence to the following six principles in virtually every recommendation, skill, or instruction regarding sales in this book. The RASSCL Principles of Persuasion are:

Reciprocation—we feel obligated to return favors performed for us

Authority—we look to experts to show us the way

Scarcity—the less available the resource the more we want it

Social Proof—we look to what others do to guide our behavior

Commitment/Consistency—we want to act consistently with our commitments and values.

Liking—the more we like people the more we want to say "yes" to them.

The Approach
One of the things I began to observe from the role-plays and from both managing sales people and monitoring hundreds of on-site sales calls was a fundamental difference in the approach some sellers used. Later I noticed how the approach of one set of sellers seemed more consistent with the RASSCL principles than the approach used by others. It was more a matter of emphasis and

the difference in emphasis made a difference in the entire sales call and, ultimately, its success. This difference was always present and though it manifested itself in different ways, it always fell into the same two categories.

I noticed that some sellers seemed to emphasize lengthy explanations about their product or company benefits and service, while others did not. Some appeared to take charge right from the outset. They followed a set plan of presentation. Others had presentations that seemed to vary from one buyer to another, and the buyer appeared to be more in charge. Some seemed ready to talk the minute the buyer stopped talking, often failing even to restrain themselves from interrupting the buyer. Others asked a lot of questions and did what they could to keep the buyer talking or merely to direct the buyer's conversation to areas that would facilitate a successful close to the sales call. The most successful sellers I studied, or have come to know (the Elite), always fell into the latter, listening vs. talking, category.

These patterns formed what I began to observe as the primary difference between successful sellers and those who were less successful. It was at the core of every sales call: listening vs. talking. I found that when talking about the product and its benefits or features was uppermost in the mind of the seller, there was little understanding of buyer needs and thus no information to help the seller know when and how to close the sale. Also, the seller was under more pressure and the pressure always seemed to show—in the seller's face or body language, in their manner, in their voice, or in their general tempo and conduct of the call.

On the other hand, when listening was at the fore, sales calls were more relaxed. There were sales calls when the product would not even be discussed, but a closing would still be offered and, miraculously in my mind, accepted by the client or buyer. Sales calls emphasizing the product explanations by the seller would last much longer, on average, and still had a lower rate of success. Those that emphasized the asking of questions would take less time, whether or not the call was a success; and I contend that spending less time in front of a buyer who isn't going to buy is just as important as spending more time in front of one who might.

Buyer Needs
So, buyer needs are the focal point, or should be, of every sales transaction. Buyer needs vary, by definition, from buyer to buyer, therefore the Elite Seller cannot presume to know each buyer's needs, but must discover them, root them out, and, most preferably, hear them expressed by the buyer in his or her own words.

Some buyers are talkative and more willing, or prone, to express their needs, frustrations, or desires. Others are reticent to do so or sometimes downright stubborn even to your most persuasive overtures or attempts to get them to talk or express themselves. You, therefore, are often without needed information—important sales information.

On the other hand, the Elite Seller has a plan, though he/she may not have a name for it, for either type of buyer. The Elite Seller begins with a presumption of cooperation and moves gradually, and only in response to buyer signals, to a strategy geared to an uncooperative or less forthcoming buyer.

Relating this back to the various sales personalities, a seller with too much Ego Drive and not enough Empathy is often using techniques that presume the buyer to be "uncooperative" even when they may not be. Ultimately, this creates an atmosphere that nurtures a lack of cooperation that causes a more argumentative environment—in essence making a cooperative buyer uncooperative. The sympathetic sales person, on the other hand, is never converting buyer expressions of need into product benefits and, of course, doesn't close the sale when the buyer's needs have been met.

Getting Around the Bases
Regardless of where you may fall, inherently, in this spectrum of skills, the overall pattern of the sales call is called (at least by me) "getting around the bases." I use this phrase because, just as in baseball, before the double play or the curve ball, you've got to master

the basics of the game—hitting the ball, catching and throwing, and touching each base in order to score runs.

There are three bases in baseball that lead runners to home plate. In Elite Selling there are three techniques that lead to a successful closing, they are: *Questioning* to uncover buyer needs; *Satisfying* buyer needs with benefits of your proposal, service, or product; and, *Closing* the sale.

Knowing when and how to perform each of these skills is another "secret" to successful selling of any kind, of any product, to anyone, anywhere. You must master these techniques, make them habitual, develop skills, language, and processes that fit with this basic pattern, to become an Elite Seller.

The three techniques again, are:

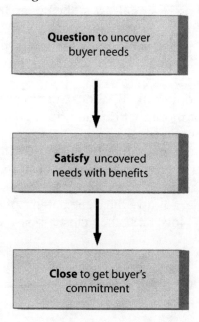

Question to uncover buyer needs

Satisfy uncovered needs with benefits

Close to get buyer's commitment

Expanding further, even if you know (or think you know) a buyer's needs, it's more motivational when you ask the buyer questions that move them to express their needs, problems, or concerns "in their own words." Then you satisfy those needs using the buyer's words when you can. Once you have satisfied enough problems, concerns, or needs, you can use the buyer's words, if you can, to attempt to close the sale. If the buyer does not accept the closing, you must determine why by, once again, asking questions followed by satisfying needs until it becomes time to close, again.

An Important Summary
This approach, the Elite Approach to selling, contrasts with other styles that promote making a mental note for each "need" a buyer reveals and then summarizing all those needs and their corresponding benefits with a lengthy explanation near the end of the call. The Elite Approach is exactly the opposite favoring a more back-and-forth method between buyer and seller; dealing with each need and solution individually. The Elite Approach is thus more conversational, allowing a discussion to move in any direction (or to change directions) according to signals from the buyer. In other words, the call moves according to what will influence the buyer to accept a closing statement, which is the goal of selling. Other benefits of this approach will be clarified as we move through the next segments.

Remember, we're only talking about "getting around the bases." There's a whole lot more that can and does go on as we round the bases, including, if you're not careful, being picked off at first base by a completely uncooperative buyer, or getting caught stealing second base if you try to close too early or in the wrong way. But, the overall goal, the essence and flow of the sales call, for the Elite and successful seller follows the basic pattern of questioning, satisfying, and closing. Now, let's take a closer look at each of these three techniques.

Chapter 7

UNCOVERING BUYER NEEDS

Obtaining buying information via a conversation is
more valuable because, in the buyer's mind,
the two of you were proceeding down a path together,
arriving at the same conclusion, together...sj

Even before the sales process begins, asking questions can be helpful to you. Asking questions is the staple of any conversation. They allow you to find out about people, to keep a conversation going, and to show your interest in what people are saying and their interests. Questions can buy some time, clarify what you don't understand, and demonstrate openness and curiosity.

Where a statement might provoke resistance ("I don't like that suggestion"), a question ("What did you think about that suggestion?") stimulates thought, prolongs the discussion, and, in sales situations, allows you to hear the buyer express themselves before you express a contrary thought that impedes your chances of success. Apart from selling, questions in the beginning of a sales call, before the selling begins, concerning the buyer's interests, hobbies, business, or life, can set the stage for questions that yield important "needs" information later in the call.

Question Statements
While this section is about "Asking Buyer Questions," questioning is just one technique used to determine what needs, problems, or concerns a buyer may have that your product, service, or proposal can satisfy. It's possible to achieve this knowledge without asking questions. Sometimes a statement, followed by a pause, is just as effective.

For example:

"There just aren't enough hours in the day to deal with all the computer problems faced by the average business"…is not a question.

But, the response could still be the answer you were looking for…

"Tell me about it; our network just crashed for the third time this month."

When statements made as part of a general conversation allow you to subtly direct the buyer to reveal problems likely to require solutions provided by your product or service, such statements are often more productive at influencing the buyer than if they resulted from a direct question from the seller. Conversation builds rapport. Rapport builds trust. Trust increases the likelihood of hearing "yes." Information obtained by virtue of a conversation is more "valuable" because in the buyers mind, the two of you were proceeding down a path together, arriving at the same conclusion, together.

Price Presumptions
Next, the term "questioning" in this context does not refer to the typical survey questions required in some sales transactions, questions of a technical nature that might be needed to fit the product to the buyer or determine a price, for example.

I recall one particular seller whose obvious talents belied her production figures. Her name was Jonnie. She seemed to know the product and she had the personality to boot, but her Closing Ratio was the worst on the team. Eventually we agreed I would accompany her for one week and see what, if anything, she was doing or saying that might account for the poor production.

It didn't take a week. Jonnie's problem was obvious in the first minute of the first sales call. She actually started each call by pulling out a survey form to begin asking questions without any regard to what the buyer had on his or her mind. And worse, the questions were based on determining a price, things like: "Let's see, how many workstations will you need?" and then, "Can I have a look at your current file server?" She was going to determine the price first so she could then begin to justify that price with offsetting features of the product.

I saw the same thing with insurance agents in my sales classes. They had a marked propensity to begin the sales process with questions like, "Now, let's see what is the construction of this building?" or "What is your total payroll?" or other questions necessary to "rate" the policy.

Of course, these questions may need to be asked, at some point, depending on the product and the applicable point of the sales cycle. But, the problem occurred because there was a basic presumption in the seller's mind that the price needed to be determined first and foremost. Since "price" was the only consideration the buyer should have, in the seller's mind, every question was therefore related to obtaining information necessary to determine the price.

In the insurance example, this often occurred when the seller knew (or thought) he/she had the best price. Such an assumption, unfortunately "presumed" the buyer was only interested in the "lowest" price, not the best deal, and worse...it ignored the fact that when the policy renewed in a year, at a higher price, the buyer had been told by the seller he/she should buy the policy that now has the lowest price instead of the one the seller was unfortunately struggling to renew.

Don't "presume" to know what's important to the buyer. Find out what's important by asking questions (or making question statements designed to elicit expressions of need) and listening to the buyer's responses, his/her words. Pay attention to the words or examples or specifics of the buyer's response. Take notes if necessary and thus show the buyer you are listening. Then, when it's time, prove you were listening by using the buyer's key words in explaining the benefit that most directly addresses their need or problem.

Types of Questions
There are two types of questions and each has its own place and time in the repertoire of an Elite Seller. Some questions are, by nature, more limiting in the responses they elicit. Others are not. Those that are more limiting are called "specific" questions. Those that are less limiting are called "general" questions.

While there are many exceptions and certainly degrees of specificity, specific questions often start with who, what, when, where, how much, how often or why. General questions, on the other hand, often begin with "Do you...," "Did you...," "Are you...," or "Have you...".

Specific questions extract small pieces of information and tend to bring the conversation to a close. General questions can piggyback on something the buyer has said with simple one word questions that can bring lengthy buyer statements, questions like "Oh?," "Really?," or "Are you kidding me?".

My catalogues of sales calls clearly showed the Elite members of our team almost always use general questions early in a sales call and continued to do so until forced to do otherwise. This allows the buyer to reveal needs in his/her own words. If the buyer doesn't reveal the needs or generally doesn't cooperate in response to the general questions, then more specific questions should gradually be utilized until the specific need or problem is revealed and quantified enough for you to introduce the benefit of your product or service that satisfies that need.

I would caution that if you find this approach tests your patience or makes you, well...anxious or "antsy" in selling situations then you are likely prone to either talk more in selling situations or to ask short, specific questions before letting the customer speak. That makes you exactly the type of seller to whom the message applies most. You must change your habits.

Before looking at a few examples of the different types of questions, let's summarize.

General Questions
General questions or statements are those that encourage the buyer to speak freely about a topic of his/her choosing or that stimulates the buyer to expand on something already stated or agreed.

Specific Questions
Specific questions or statements are those that steer the sales conversation to specific topics of your choosing and limits buyer responses (sometimes to short one or two-word answers), usually in topic areas you have chosen.

Now, let's contrast the two types of questions via several examples.

Example one:

> General Question: "I believe you mentioned problems with your current system, can you tell me about some of those problems?"

> Specific Questions: "Do the problems you mentioned with your current system have to do with service call response time?"

Example two (questions in statement form):

> General: "We hear a lot of complaints from people about their property insurance coverage."

Specific: "Most of our new clients were using systems that were unable to promise them same day repair service."

It's important to note that, whether using the statement approach or the question approach and whether or not you use the option of a specific question or a more general one, the goal is the same—to discover the buyer problem or need so that you can introduce a product feature that satisfies that need. It's important that this be done in the context and in response to the buyer statement rather than just blurting it out without knowing, or having only presumed, it to be a real need of the buyer.

In my experience, this is a key difference between those who make sales calls and those who make sales. The Elite Seller understands that a buyer is more accepting of something you say if it is in direct response to something he/she just said they wanted or must have.

Many times I've witnessed a sales person who explained a product feature, even an extremely competitive price, be put in the position of having to defend why the benefit was important. In response to:

"We've got the lowest price in town," the buyer was non-committal, even uninterested in the lowest price as indicated by the following response:

"Price isn't the most important consideration in making a decision of this magnitude." To which the appropriate response from the seller was...

"What do you consider to be the most important consideration?" that lead to other benefits the buyer needed.

This enables the sales person to have benefit of those "benefits" when the buyer either brings up the price later on or discovers that your competitor has an even lower price.

Chapter 8

RIGHT QUESTIONS, RIGHT TIME

Using words the buyer uses builds rapport. Rapport builds trust.
Trust increases the likelihood of hearing "yes"...sj

Okay, so there are two types of questions or need gathering statements, general and specific. The general statement or question is more apt to allow the buyer to direct the conversation to areas where he/she will reveal meaningful buyer needs. A specific question or statement is less likely to do so, and, even if it does, often results in fewer words or verbiage in the buyer's response. Those buyer words and verbiage are important for the seller to have—very important.

Remember, buyer words are what you're after. They are the nuggets of success. The more you hear, the more tools you have with which to shape your responses. Buyer words can be used to summarize needs and to point to product features that truly satisfy those needs in a way the buyer can relate to. Using words the buyer uses, builds rapport. Rapport builds trust. Trust increases the likelihood of hearing "yes."

Therefore, in all matters, opt for general questions. Begin with general questions and follow up buyer comments with the most general question you can think of. My favorite is the simple phrase "Oh?" Or, sometimes "Really?" is good.

Let's take the previous example from above and expand on it.

After some initial conversation, the seller begins to channel the call in a purposeful direction with a statement of general need.

> Seller: "You know, our other customers are telling us more and more that it's getting so there just aren't enough hours in the day to deal with all the system problems faced by the average business."

> Buyer: "Tell me about it; our network just crashed for the third time this month."

> Seller: "Oh?"

> Buyer: "Yeah, we've been down almost seven days total and it's costing us a bundle; I don't know if we can keep this up much longer without making some adjustments."

In this example the simple question "oh?" generated very valuable information. The buyer's business, or portions of it, has been down seven days because of network crashes. They've lost money because of it. They are already considering some changes or adjustments.

In response, there are many options the seller can now take, including questions of either a general or specific nature, or even the less recommended approach of explaining a benefit related to system crashes. But, the point is, the options came as a result of the seller not assuming to know what systems problems the buyer was having and instead opting for the most general of questions, encouraging the buyer to speak more freely.

Let's continue the conversation above.

In response to the buyer saying, "Yeah, we've been down almost seven days total and it's costing us a bundle; I don't know if we can keep this up much longer without making some adjustments," the seller has three reasonable options:

1.) a general question;

2.) a specific question; or,

3.) a statement designed to satisfy the buyer's problem (covered in the next segment).

The Elite Seller would instinctively opt for number one, the Ego Driven seller for number three, and number two is a fairly neutral option, but less desirable than number one.

Here is a sample for each of the three possible responses:

1.) General question: "Oh?" or the correct, but less desirable, "What kind of adjustments?"

2.) Specific question: "Is one of the adjustments under consideration the purchase of a new network system?"

3.) Need satisfying statement: "That's why we have a complete 24-hour repair service that will respond within 45 minutes of your call, day or night, guaranteed."

So, why did I say that "oh?" was a more preferred question in the example above than "What kind of adjustments?" Again, because "oh?" is the more general of the two and wasn't conversationally inappropriate or awkward.

Now, to illustrate the value of using the more general approach, let's look at possible buyer responses based on the differing seller approaches—one, two, or three above.

Using approach number one above where the seller merely says "Oh?", the buyer said:

> "That's right. And, just like their guarantee, the repair person was always here within the hour, but...the system never stayed fixed for long. I think they need that same day service guarantee because they know their software design still has so many bugs."

37

This response should bring home the point of the Elite Seller approach; that is, opting for the most general question or statement is far more preferred. Asking "What kind of system?" (instead of saying "oh?"), could've yielded something unrelated to purchasing a new system, dealing merely with fixing the current one. Had approach number two been used, the answer would've been:

"No, we aren't considering buying a new network system."

While option two wasn't the most preferred approach, the buyer response immediately above could at least be followed with another general question along the lines of the first. Perhaps something like...

"Really?" or "What are you considering?" or "Why not?"

But, had approach number three, the Ego Driven approach, been used, the seller would've actually lost ground by stating something his product offered that the buyer's current system (with which there was dissatisfaction) also offered, a same day service guarantee. Remember, this feature of the buyer's current system not only wasn't solving the buyer's problem, it was actually a signal to the buyer that there might be software bugs.

An Important Recap
The most general question is almost always the most appropriate, especially early in the call. It shows you're interested in what the buyer is saying and it motivates buyers by letting them talk. General questions not only give the seller more precise information about buyer needs, they give the seller the words the buyer uses to describe those needs—a veritable gold mine for closing the sales call.

If general questions have been used in the beginning, rapport is often built and trust is established. In other words, the seller is earning the right to take tighter control of the conversation, to use more specific questions to direct the sales call or even to introduce a benefit without using questions at all. In fact, it can become quite natural for specific questions to begin flowing as the sales call progresses. With rapport and trust established, each party can behave more naturally and conversationally, allowing a free exchange of information and creating the most ideal selling (and closing) environment.

Chapter 9

INTRODUCING BENEFITS
We first make our habits, and then our habits
make us...John Dryden

So, the question now is "What do you do once, as the result of a line of general then perhaps more specific questions, you finally hear the buyer express a need for a feature of your product or service?" Obviously, it's time to introduce and/or describe the benefit that answers or solves the buyers expressed need. But, Elite Sellers do this using a Specific Benefit Statement that maximizes the persuasive impact by using two steps to introduce the benefit. Why two steps? Why not just describe the benefit that solves the customer's problem?

Behavioral scientist Ellen Langer and her team of researchers launched a series of studies designed to test the power of the word "because." That is, what is the persuasive impact of providing a reason for a request being made of someone else? A simple question really. Most people would naturally assume that providing the rationale or the reason for a request would increase the chances of hearing the favorable response..."yes!" In the first phase of her study Langer hired a stranger to attempt to get ahead of others waiting in line to use the Xerox machine at a large corporation. They

41

were instructed to merely say…"Excuse me, I have five pages. May I use the Xerox machine?"

Faced with this basic request to cut in line, 60 percent of those approached agreed to allow the stranger to go ahead. But…when the stranger gave a reason, "May I use the Xerox machine because I'm in a rush?" almost everyone complied — 94 percent said "yes!"

Again, not surprising that a rational reason generated greater acceptance of the request. But, Langer's next survey was truly enlightening. The stranger used the word "because," but followed it with a completely meaningless reason. The results? They were still in the 94 percent range. Specifically, the stranger said…. "May I use the Xerox machine, because I have to make copies?"

Subconsciously, the employee would've thought "Of course you have to make copies, but that's not a reason for me to let you go first." Nonetheless, despite the irrational nature of the stranger's logic, the mere attempt to justify the request generated the same level of success. In other words, the request was more persuasive than the request with no rationale, even with obviously flawed logic.

This is why many of the skills in Platform I used to introduce benefits or to handle difficult buyers will require the Elite Seller to make an additional step: to "rephrase," "expand," or "summarize" a buyer's statements before requesting a commitment of the buyer or before introducing a benefit. These steps also embrace the "Liking" principle and they foster communication in furtherance of other RASSCL Principles such as #5 — Commitment/Consistency and #1 — Reciprocation.

Specific Benefit Statement
Therefore, what do you do when and if, as the result of a line of general then perhaps more specific questions, you finally hear the buyer express a need for a feature of your product or service? Keeping in mind the Langer study, the Elite Seller introduces the benefit using a Specific Benefit Statement that has two steps, as follows:

1.) Expand on the buyer's need. You do this by agreeing and/or repeating the need or problem using the buyer's language (if you can) to both expand and confirm its importance. Then,

2.) Introduce the appropriate benefit or feature that solves or answers the need.

Let's take a look at how this works by continuing the conversation regarding the feature of same day service from the previous chapter.

Seller: "You know, it's getting so there just aren't enough hours in the day to deal with all the system problems faced by the average business."

Buyer: "Tell me about it; our network just crashed for the third time this month."

Seller: "Oh?"

Buyer: "Yeah, we've been down almost seven days total and it's costing us a bundle, I don't know if we can keep this up much longer, not without making some adjustments."

Seller: "Really?"

Buyer: "That's right. And, just like their guarantee, the repair person was always here within the hour, but…their system never stayed fixed for long. I think the only reason they guarantee same day service is because they know their software still has so many bugs."

Seller: "What do you mean?"

Buyer: "Well, it figures doesn't it? Market pressure being what it is, they probably needed to release the software sooner than planned, knowing it still had a few bugs in it. You know; to beat the competition out of the gate. They figured they could fix any glitches after the software was installed in a buyer's office. Let's face it; wouldn't it be better to guarantee that nothing would go wrong rather than guarantee that when it does you'll fix it? I should've seen their one day guarantee as a sign they had bugs rather than as a sign for good service."

The Elite Seller should immediately recognize this opportunity to make a Specific Benefit Statement.

First, expanding on the buyer's need, the seller says:

"You're absolutely right! Actually that happens quite often in the software industry; it's called the fix the glitch approach to product development. Instead of adequate beta testing, they figure to beat the competition to market and worry about repairing glitches on-site, making you the beta test site.

Now, having laid out the rationale for the existence of the feature and thus the benefit, step two of the Specific Benefit Statement—that of introducing the appropriate benefit—is more easily accepted by the buyer when rendered as follows:

"At ACME software, we would never waste your time and money that way. We have an extensive beta testing process, which, along with a decade of upgrades, enables us to guarantee you won't encounter any bugs in our software. Our promise of same day service is for hardware problems or additional training or enhancements, not for software bugs in a system that doesn't have any..."

Buyer: "Hmm...I wish the vendor of our current system had used that approach."

At this point, the seller can continue with this line of questioning, expanding on the benefit of "no bugs," or the seller can move on to other subjects using general then more specific questioning techniques or, depending on cues from the buyer, he/she could attempt to close the sale.

This seller, however, feels he/she needs at least one more benefit on the table before attempting to close, so the following general question is asked by the seller:

> "Tell me, what other problems have you had with your current system?"

> Buyer: "Well, it's been running a little slow lately."

> Seller: "Really?"

> Buyer: "Well, yes. Activities that we used to get done in an hour are now taking almost an entire morning. The system takes so long to migrate from one function to another that we spend all our time staring at the screen and drumming our fingers on the desk."

> Seller: "Does this impact more than just the time spent on individual tasks?"

> Buyer: "You bet it does! We're actually spending more time making entries and printing reports than we are selling product. I can't afford to have both data entry and salespeople. I need to have salespeople making their own entries and if that takes too long, well…they aren't in front of buyers."

The seller, again immediately recognizes the opportunity to make another Specific Benefit Statement.

Expanding the buyer's need first, the seller says:

> "I agree with you one hundred percent! You need to have sellers selling, not wasting their time and your money making data entries for the accounting department."

Now, with step two, the seller can introduce the benefit with maximum impact:

"Our sysem was actually designed by salespeople, so they can update while they are on the road, in half the time of any other system on the market today. Our beta testing was in the field on actual sales calls with salespeople from several different industries, including yours."

Buyer: "Hmmm…that sounds pretty good. But, how do I know I can afford all this functionality?"

At this point, the seller may conclude that a request for pricing information is a signal to close the sale. Or, he/she might conclude that it is a question which must first be answered. The point is, that general questions were used to lead the buyer to make statements that the seller could use, not only to justify making a Specific Benefit Statement, but to customize it to the buyer's specific situation.

And again, information obtained by virtue of a conversation is more influencing, because, in the buyer's mind, the two of you were proceeding down a path together, arriving at the same conclusion, together.

Plus, the opportunity to offer a benefit of the product isn't squandered with a casual response like, "we can do that" or "we offer that benefit." By using the Specific Benefit Statement, the benefit is expanded and customized for persuasive impact as indicated by the Langer study—expanded to seem larger and more important, customized so that it appears to be specifically for "this" buyer or buyers just like this one. The phrases or sentences you use in making a Specific Benefit Statement should use the words of the buyer in answering your questions as much as possible. How can a buyer argue or deny the benefit when they just said they had a problem it satisfies and when you used their own language in describing it? Answer: they can't!

The Phase Approach
A question that often occurs (and that I referenced in the previous chapter) as a result of the dialogue above is whether or not it is appropriate to store up buyer needs or problems rather than answer

46

each need as it is expressed. In other words, do Elite Sellers use the "phase" approach to selling, spending the early part (or opening phase) of the call asking questions and gathering information and the latter part (or closing phase) showing the buyer how their product satisfies the numerous needs uncovered in the beginning phase?

The answer, in my experience, is that Elite Sellers almost always handle each expression of need as it arises. Consistent with numerous RASSCL principles, this is more conversational because you aren't just asking a line of questions or interrogating the buyer. The Elite Approach is not only more conversational (and thus motivational) for the buyer, but it fits with the closing statement we'll see in the next section, which is structured to include a "summary" of benefits. Because a closing "summary" occurs right before you request a buyer commitment, it accomplishes the same benefit of the closing phase in the phase approach to selling; only without the drawbacks often encountered in the opening phase of the phase approach.

Chapter 10

CLOSING THE SALE

If you've done a good job asking questions and introducing benefits, then closing the sale is the next logical step for both seller & buyer...sj

Unfortunately, the time for closing a sale is not always obvious. That's why many sellers either do it too soon, to late, or...not at all. Referring back to the opening chapter on Ego and Empathy, those with more Ego than Empathy often close too soon. Those with too much Empathy sometimes never close. Ego driven individuals aren't concerned about buyer needs and signals, only with their own need to make the sale. Empathetic individuals often sympathize with the buyer's desire to not spend money so much so that they never even ask them to. Their fear of rejection often dominates their actions in selling situations.

Let's talk about the fear factor first.

I once took a sales course in which students spent the entire morning learning how to close and how to overcome the fear of rejection at this most important point of a sales call. Nothing else was discussed. Seemingly, nothing else mattered. During one hour long segment, the entire class divided into groups of two with instructions to close imaginary sales and refuse to take no for an answer.

No matter what the excuse, come up with another reason for the buyer to buy, we were told. And, so we did, for one full hour, over and over again.

It was a bit frustrating; especially for those with Empathy so bountiful that they would not have closed in the first place, but…it was a very educational exercise. It actually was useful in removing reluctance and fear and thus transforming some high Empathy "nonclosers" into better closers. It did this by helping them build a new habit—the habit of asking for something even when you "know," or think you know, you aren't going to get it, or when your fear of rejection has convinced you that you won't get it.

What about those who close too early or too often?

In knowing when to close a sales call, it may be important to think of RASSCL Principle #5, Commitment/Consistency. People, generally, want to appear consistent, reasonable, and committed to those things they espouse. While waiting too long to close, or failing to catch a buying signal from a buyers is undesirable, science tells us it is preferable to closing to early. By definition, an early close is one that is not accepted by the buyer. According to the RASSCL Principle of Consistency you have now placed the buyer in the position of defending that decision; perhaps through the rest of the sales call.

My friend Alex Soto told me a personal story that goes direct to this point. As a civic-minded citizen with noted leadership qualities, Alex was summoned for jury duty and, in short order, nominated to be the foreman. When the trial ended and deliberations began, he figured a good way to "shake things out" was to ask for a straw vote before any discussion; it might, after all, save time if everyone agreed on the first vote. Unfortunately, everyone didn't agree. This left those in the minority, and those in the majority, defending their opening vote, even when confronted with overwhelming evidence to the contrary. In this instance, if memory serves, guilty was the appropriate verdict. But, those favoring "innocence" argued bitterly…more because they had to justify the vote they were publicly forced to make when the jury foreman had, in essence, "closed" too early.

The Elite Seller closes, without regard to fear of rejection, and without regard to anything other than buying signals from the buyer and the natural flow of the sales call. It is more the latter, the logical flow of the sales call (with one exception applying to extreme indifference), that guides an Elite Seller. Buying signals can be interpreted differently by different sellers, but they often occur after introducing a benefit or two or after handling a difficult objection, which we'll discuss in the section on buyer attitudes. Buying signals are often the same as "tells" in poker except it's rare that they are anything other than something the buyer says as opposed to some subtle body language or facial tick.

Either way, your closing statement is extremely important; its structure, your attitude, and what you do and say immediately following are key to sales success. Like introducing benefits with a Specific Benefit Statement and consistent with the RASSCL principles, there are two steps to a closing statement.

1.) Summarize the benefits of your product or service the buyer agreed to during the call.

2.) Request the appropriate commitment.

Let's look in more detail at each step. In step one, assuming you've followed the previous steps in the Elite Approach, you summarize the benefits that you and the buyer have agreed your product or service can deliver. In actuality you are only closing because it is imminently logical and consistent (RASSCL Principle #5) for you to do so.

After all, you used general questions to allow the buyer to tell you his/her needs. You confirmed and expanded those needs as the first step in your benefit statements, immediately prior to showing the buyer how you can provide the needed benefit. Based on having done that for one, and maybe two or three benefits, you don't need any "red flag" buying signals (whatever you may consider them to be). The only logical and consistent thing for you to do is give the buyer information on how to get the benefits he/she has said were important and that he/she has agreed your product can provide.

Assumptive Close

Following this logic, it is therefore consistent and helpful that positive language be used. Everything you say should reflect the "assumption" that the sale is made and that only the details of how, when, or how much are left to decide. And being a seller that uses the Elite approach, you'll even give the buyer a choice of how to buy the product or service if you can.

Here's how a sample summary of benefits might sound.

> "Mr. Johnson, let me see if I've got all we've agreed to. You said that having a system adequately tested and proven to be free of software bugs is important, both in saving time and in keeping your sales people out on the road calling on buyers. We agreed that Acme's software package is far superior in this regard.
>
> You also mentioned that processing speed is important, especially when it comes to keeping down costs and improving production. I showed you information that proved Acme has one of the fastest processors in the business and that our unique programs operate more efficiently."

By summarizing the benefits, you've cemented the buyer's agreement and made it more difficult to refuse to give you a commitment. By summarizing each benefit agreed to, you've given the buyer "two dimes and a nickel" instead of a quarter; that is, instead of saying something like, "You can see it's what you're looking for," you itemized each reason that it's what the buyer is looking for. Again, in keeping with RASSCL Principle #5, buyers want to appear consistent; you're only giving him/her what they said they wanted, not what you thought or assumed they needed.

The Positive Sale

About the time that illnesses first began to be linked to a person's mental outlook and the term psychosomatic began to emerge, a doctor in Geneva Switzerland named Émile Coué began telling each of his patients to repeat, over and over the phrase, "Every day, in every way, I'm getting better and better." Initially scoffed at, Dr.

Coué's results could not be so easily dismissed. His rate of cure was five times higher than that of other similar clinics for patients with similar ailments. That was 1895.

Later, in 1905, a German doctor expanded on Dr. Coué's work with something he called "Autogenic Conditioning" wherein he mixed relaxation, aural statements of health by the patients and creative visualizations to reprogram their subconscious. Dr. Johannes Schultz's work spread rapidly to Europe and to the professions of teaching and athletic competition. Dr. Norman Vincent Peale was the first to apply the concept to the business world.

Creative images and positive language can be a powerful influence on customers as well. While it can be overdone, it's not a bad idea to use both throughout the sales call. There are certain words that presume a sale is imminent or at least logical. You can develop the habit of saying "when" instead of "if." For example, "When you have our network system, Mr. Jones, you also will have our guarantee of first rate service." Or, "When you buy a policy from the XYZ Agency, you're buying peace of mind."

Conversely, negative words can have a dampening effect. The word "if" raises the possibility of not buying from you or not buying your product. It tells the buyer that even the seller thinks it's reasonable to assume that a sale might not be possible. The buyer may begin thinking "Maybe I should buy it or maybe I shouldn't" when he hears the word. He may even begin to use the word himself in describing his decision, with something like "If I were to buy this, and I'm not saying I will, then…" or "If I buy from you, and frankly that's a big if, then I'll need…" etc.

You can also begin to develop the habit of using the first person plural "we" and "let's." For example, "We should make certain that you are insured 100 percent to value" or "Let's not forget that we can finance that premium for you in-house." This use of "we," "us," and "our" also helps the prospect develop the idea that he/she won't be making an important decision entirely on their own; they'll have an experts help, RASSCL Principle #2. People, most people, feel better making decisions with someone else because the responsibility is not solely on their shoulders (RASSCL Principle #4).

Positive Transitioning

Being positive during the close is so important it's often a good idea to have or to practice several transitions to summarizing the benefits. Here are the top ten I've collected, but you may know others or be able to find them from hundreds of publications. My only goal, for you, is that you have just a few that you feel comfortable using and which you develop the habit of using.

"Let's see if there's anything we missed by reviewing what we've agreed to up to this point."

"Why don't we take a moment and see how many of the things we discussed actually fit your situation. Would that be okay?"

"Wow, that's a lot to digest in such a short time. Can we take a few moments to make sure I've got everything?"

"Okay, forgetting details for a minute, let's look at the big picture."

"Before you make up your mind one way or another, let's make sure we're in the ballpark."

"Before we forget something, let's jot down where we are. Is that okay with you?"

"We've covered a lot of areas today. Would it be all right with you if we reviewed the highlights of this proposal?"

"It sounds like we've got the best deal for you, but let's be sure by rechecking what we've discussed."

"At the risk of sounding redundant, here's what I think are the highlights of today's meeting."

"Okay, we've come a long way. Let's see just how far by recapping for a second."

Any one of the above statements could be used for a wide variety of products or services. They may not fit exactly to your product and certainly not to every situation. The point is to use them as a guide for developing one or two that fit your product or service. Write them out if you need to. Practice saying them in a wide variety of situations. Develop a mental process for mixing in words that you heard the buyer use during the sales call. Build the habit!

A Positive Commitment

Here's an example of how to use the positive approach, giving your buyer options, when you ask for the check or request the appropriate commitment.

> "It would appear that Acme has just what the doctor ordered for both your internal and external software problems. We have a special right now which includes free installation and training when you schedule an installation and put down a deposit before March the second. Assuming you want to save that money, which month is better for your installation, January or February?"

As I said, after the Summary of Benefits, it is imminently logical to ask for the order or the commitment, whatever that may be. At this point it is absolutely imperative that you not vary from the game plan, which is to assume the sale has been made. Here again, are the top ten examples I've kept over the years of how to ask for the order while assuming the sale is made:

> "It's clear you know a good deal when you hear it. Why don't we go ahead and give it to you so you can share it with your staff this afternoon?"

> "Well, to receive all the benefits we just agreed to, we need to close the contract. Let me show you where to sign and we can schedule our training after that."

> "When would you like us to move on this, right before the holidays or when you get back from vacation?"

"Isn't this the kind of overall cost benefit you were looking for? I thought so. All you have to do is sign here and we begin working for you."

"Considering these benefits, the main question for you is working an installation date into your busy schedule. I would suggest sooner so as to begin enjoying the advantages now."

"Since we've had such wide agreement on the benefits, why not make it effective on May the first?"

"Okay, how do you want to pay for this; one upfront lump sum or, if you prefer, we can arrange to have the premium financed for you?"

"This plan fits like a glove. At the risk of sounding presumptuous, how much of a down payment fits your budget?"

"There you have it, five compelling reasons to buy our plan. Would you like to hear one more, our early installation discount?"

"Okay, let's start with your signature here on the contract and then there on a check for the initial deposit."

Again, any one of the above statements could be used for a wide variety of products or services. They may not fit exactly to your product and certainly not to every situation. The point is to use them as a guide for developing one or two that fit your product or service. Write them out. Practice saying them in a wide variety of situations. Develop a mental process for using words that you heard the buyer use during the sales call. Build the habit!

After the Closing
We've all heard the saying that the best thing to say after you have requested a commitment or have made your closing statement is nothing at all. Don't do or say anything that allows the buyer the opportunity to rid him or herself of the burden to choose between "yes, I will buy" or "no, I'm not ready to buy." Anything you do or say can provide the opportunity for someone to wiggle out of spending money, even when it's in their best interests.

Of course, it isn't always as easy as it sounds, remaining silent when you're the one that's supposed to be in charge of the conversation. But, I subscribe to the theory that silence after the closing statement is paramount. Let the buyer break the silence.

You're liable to find several possible responses if you allow them to be made. They'll usually fall into one of the three following categories:

1.) An indication from the buyer that they are not ready to buy.

2.) An indication from the buyer that they may be willing to buy, but need more information before doing so.

3.) No relevant response or silence.

Rarely did I observe a buyer's response to a request for commitment or a closing statement fall outside of these three options. And, though we haven't even begun to discuss the various buyer attitudes and how to handle each one of them, we have already learned the pattern of seller responses to these three possible buyer reactions.

In response to number one, an indication from the buyer that they are not ready to buy, the seller needs to determine what the problem is or why the buyer is not willing to "sign on the dotted line" so to speak. The best way to do this is to ask a general question and allow the buyer to speak freely about what's on their mind. One good example is "what's the problem?" Another is "what's wrong?" Or, depending on how they said they weren't ready a simple "oh?" will often suffice.

The point is you begin at first base, asking general questions that will tell you what you need to know in order to satisfy the need, which you failed to uncover with your previous questions. Of course, it's likely at this point, when confronted with making a commitment that may include actually spending some money, that the buyer has an objection, perhaps a serious one, which you failed to uncover. An objection is a special type of buyer attitude that needs to be handled in a specific way. We'll talk about how to handle buyer attitudes in a subsequent section.

Of course, it may be that the buyer's response to your request for a commitment falls more in line with number two above; they may be willing to buy, but need more information before making a commitment. If so, they will state that information and you will provide the information requested to the best of your ability. This could lead to another abbreviated closing, to a signing of the deal, or to an objection or other buyer attitude that must be handled.

If the third category of response, "no relevant response or silence," is encountered, then it's likely you'll have to ask specific questions to take tighter control, limit answers, and uncover any problems or hidden attitudes. But, be careful to allow the buyer to break any interval of silence.

Then, when you hear the response, act accordingly by either asking a general or specific question, handling the attitude as described in subsequent chapters, or by closing the sale, again, perhaps by abbreviating your closing statement the second, or possibly, a third time.

Either way, that's all there is to "Getting Around the Bases" —basically three steps as outlined earlier: merely asking questions, satisfying needs, and closing the sale.

Repeat Business
It's great to do business with existing and satisfied customers. Closing the sale for "repeat" or "renewal" business is almost always easier and you should use the "assumptive" words we've been discussing, but avoid making the customer feel like they are being taken for granted.

For example, a software seller reminds the customer that he/she needs to keep in mind that "More storage space may be needed this year the way you keep growing." The insurance seller says, "We want to be sure and allow for inflation and the increase cost of building materials when we set your coverage limit over the next policy term." Again, the language used assumes the sale but doesn't indicate the buyer is being taken for granted. It does this by dealing with ways to improve the product offering during the coming year or product term. It's about the buyer's needs and, since those needs can be satisfied by you and since you've proven your worth during the previous year, it's logical to assume the sale is made for another year.

GETTING AROUND THE BASES

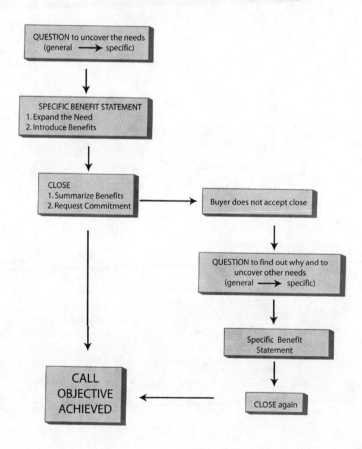

Chapter 11

DIRECTING THE SALES CALL
Make good habits and they will make you...Parks Cousins

In handling difficult buyers, it's often necessary to take tighter control of the sales call and to direct the buyer to subject areas of your choosing. The subject areas will depend on many factors that only the seller can decide based on facts and circumstances of the call. However, the structure for dealing with various buyer attitudes, discussed in the next chapter, will usually involve either asking questions, usually specific questions, or making various types of benefit statements.

Remember in Chapter 9 that Specific Benefit Statements were made when the buyer expressed a need or problem as the result of questions (maybe a question statement or two) from the seller? Usually, the questions were first general and then, if necessary, they became more specific.

Though this general-to-specific questioning technique is the preferred method, my sales team and I often discussed other ways that were appropriate or beneficial in getting buyers to express a specific need. After all, they said, "not every situation calls for a long line of questioning from the seller" and for various reasons the seller may wish or need to introduce benefits in another way.

As we saw in a previous chapter it is possible to obtain buyer information without using questions, but by using Question Statements. These can be short statements like,

> "In this lawsuit happy world, it's a wonder anyone can run a business."

This statement from an insurance seller was designed to elicit, hopefully, a buyer comment that might reveal a need that could be satisfied by the purchase of a Commercial Umbrella Liability Policy. Unfortunately, when rendered by itself the statement may or may not have the desired impact.

As you can see, the link between the seller's statement and the "desired" response is not clear enough to guarantee an appropriate (or any) buyer statement will be made. In situations where you want the buyer to express needs without using questions (or Question Statements), you can use what's called a General Benefit Statement.

And, in keeping with the lessons of the Langer study and the benefit of the word "because," there are two steps in a General Benefit Statement:

1.) Describe an assumed general need; then,

2.) Answer that need with a general benefit of your product or service.

This differs from a Specific Benefit Statement because it is rendered before the buyer has expressed a specific need and you must, therefore, assume a need exists in order to cause the buyer to express a specific need you can answer with a Specific Benefit Statement.

For example, using the Commercial Umbrella Liability Policy example above, the seller could've described an assumed need by saying something like:

> "In today's litigious society, it's important for every business to have security from frivolous lawsuits. Just a single one million dollar judgment and you could be out of business."

Then, step two is to answer the need with something like:

> "That's why we recommend, just to be on the safe side, that all of our customers purchase a Commercial Umbrella Policy. That way you know both your judgment and defense costs will be taken care of no matter what you are being sued for."

At this point the seller waits for a response, maybe a question, from the buyer. Something like:

> "Really, an Umbrella policy...I thought all I needed was the General Liability and Commercial Auto Fleet policies you sold me."

At this point the insurance seller can ask a question or make a Specific Benefit Statement citing a specific need along the lines of the following:

> "You're right to be concerned about adequate liability protection. Fact is, not every policy provides everything for every situation. Sometimes it's more efficient to use the umbrella approach to complement both uncovered items and the limited amounts of coverage provided by your underlying policies. With an umbrella, you'll have all the peace of mind you need and can focus on making money for your business, not worrying about frivolous lawsuits."

At this point, depending on the buyer's response, the seller can begin to explain how an "Umbrella" policy works and cite additional examples of when one might be needed. Or, he/she can resume the Elite Approach of asking questions like:

> "Are you familiar with what can happen if one of your delivery personnel were to cause an accident because they were, heaven forbid, under the influence of drugs or alcohol?"

Hopefully, at this point the buyer becomes engaged with the seller, listening and questioning, while the seller explains and asks questions about what can happen and, via Specific Benefit Statements, what can be done to protect against the devastation of a lawsuit, frivolous or otherwise.

Initial Benefit Statements
Often, in the beginning of a sales call a series of questions can be awkward or can put off a customer. I discovered some Elite Sellers who would begin by making general type benefit statements in order to segue into the sales process without the use of questions or question statements. Sometimes a busy or "harried" buyer might try to "get down to business" with a statement like:

"Okay, what have you got for me?" Or,

"Now, what can I do for you today?" or something equally effective at getting the seller to begin, well…selling.

In such situations, statements may work better than questions. Statements of this nature, made at the beginning of a sales call are called Initial Benefit Statements. They are the same as General Benefit Statements, but used at the beginning, "initially."

The key with either a General or Initial Benefit Statement is to keep it general so as to allow the customer to respond with details, using their own words. Then, you can encourage them to talk with general questions followed by specific questions if necessary. And finally, when you hear the specific need expressed, you use a Specific Benefit Statement to introduce a specific benefit by:

1.) Expanding the customer's need, problem, or concern; and,

2.) Introducing the benefit that solves that need, problem, or concern.

An Important Summary
Again, there are four types of benefit statements sellers can use to "direct" the sales call, depending on preference, timing, and cues from the customer.

Directing the Sales Call

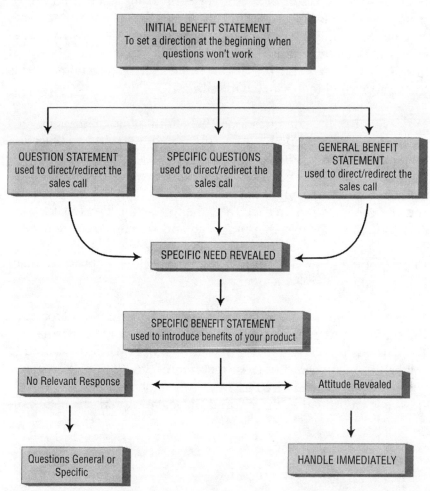

During the sales call, the Specific Benefit Statement is preferred because it is the result of the buyer expressing a specific need or problem in his/her own words. This allows the seller to offer a specific benefit using the buyer's words if possible. That's why a Specific Benefit Statement usually occurs at the end of a line of general questions followed, if necessary, by more specific questions. This is the preferred, Elite Approach to selling.

However, the line of questions that culminated with a buyer's statement of need could have begun instead with either a Question Statement, an Initial Benefit Statement (made at the beginning of the sales call), or a General Benefit Statement made during the sales call when questions might not be working or there is a need to redirect the conversation. In each case, the use of questions to steer the sales call were deemed inappropriate and statements were used— Initial, General, or Question Statements—merely to lead the buyer to say something that could warrant a Specific Benefit Statement being made, which is the goal.

In essence, with these options for introducing benefits and for causing the buyer to express needs or problems the Elite Seller has the tools necessary to adapt to any selling situation. Once you build the habit of using each of these techniques, you'll have a complete arsenal from which to extract whatever is needed and to "direct" the sales call towards the desired objective. Again, all it takes is practice!

Chapter 12

HANDLING BUYER ATTITUDES
**Always think in terms of what the other person
wants...James Van Fleet**

To this point, we've covered the techniques of selling to a buyer that is relatively cooperative. They believe us, they are polite, they respond when we ask them questions, and...they listen, understand, and even agree with our solutions. Hardly realistic. The challenge of persuading someone under such circumstances is significantly diminished and rarely reflects what most sellers encounter in the real world. In fact, if the buyer doesn't cop at least one of a number of attitudes during the average sales call, you really aren't engaged in influencing or persuading (selling); rather, you are engaged merely in sharing information with someone about your product or service and perhaps, hopefully, explaining how much they have to pay to get it.

RASSCL Principles II
However, selling is about influencing or persuading others—that is, convincing someone to do something they aren't otherwise inclined to do. In Chapter 6, I referenced the six universal Principles of Persuasion. Let's take another look at the Principles of Persuasion (RASSCL) in the context of handling buyer attitudes.

1.) **Reciprocation**—people feel obligated to return favors. For example, a seller explains that he or she won't waste the buyer's time with irrelevant information or sales fluff and will provide only facts if the buyer will not waste the seller's time by asking him to come back later before making a buying decision or by not having all decision makers in the room.

2.) **Authority**—people look to experts to give them direction and to help in making decisions. For example, the seller is accredited in his field with professional designations and, rather than a "sales pitch" approach, he/she uses a more consultative style (the Elite style) with clients and buyers. The seller offers independent proof of important benefits.

3.) **Scarcity**—the less available the resource, the more someone wants it. The seller shows the downside of procrastinating, when the buyer says "I'd like to think it over," by revealing a special for those who purchase now, or that installation will be delayed if not done before a certain time, or that there are only limited quantities available.

4.) **Social Proof**—people look to what others do, or have done, to guide their behavior and their decisions. For example, the seller provides testimonials from satisfied buyers about his/her service and company performance. The seller references the actions of others similar to the buyer at key points in the sales call.

5.) **Commitment/Consistency**—people want to appear to act consistently with their commitments and values. For example, just like your questions and benefit statement happen only after the buyer states a need, summarizing benefits in your closing statement makes it logical and consistent (and easier) for the buyer to say "yes." These techniques are particularly helpful, as you'll see, in handling difficult objections via Benjamin Franklin's "Ledger" approach.

6.) **Liking**—the more buyers like someone, the more they want to say "yes" to that someone. The seller persuades without being "pushy" by using questions, general to specific, to uncover buyer needs. The seller shows the customer he/she is listening by rephrasing, summarizing, and clarifying buyer statements and objections. And, as I've said before, "Using words the buyer uses builds rapport. Rapport builds trust. Trust increases the likelihood of hearing yes!"

Matching & Mirroring

If it hasn't already become apparent, much of the emphasis in Elite Selling is on improved communication by rephrasing, restating, expanding, summarizing, or confirming what buyers have said or what you and the buyer have agreed to. This builds rapport, which increases trust, which helps the buyer say "Yes!" Not only did I see this firsthand from the top sellers on my sales team, the effectiveness of this approach is scientifically substantiated and has been a basic principle in the psychology of persuasion for decades.

For example, restaurants have long provided a high volume, controlled environment for testing various face-to-face sales techniques. While the food, service, atmosphere, and other factors can influence repeat business, usually the food server's success is measured by how much he/she receives in tips as a percentage of sales when compared to other waiters and waitresses in the same restaurant. Informally, servers report that they get higher tips, for example, if they simply repeat orders back to every customer. Under scientifically controlled conditions, research by Rick van Baarne tested this idea. He found that food servers who restated customer orders received over 70 percent more in gratuities than those who did not. Again, this was for the same volume of sales.

The results are consistent not only with the RASSCL Principles, but with similar research from social psychologists, Tanya Chartrand and John Bargh, who found that merely matching the behavior of others creates feelings of "liking " and strengthens the bonds between two people meeting for the first time. In fact, their tests of matching body language confirmed that it's not just saying the words of others, but reflecting their posture and mannerisms that also causes people to be liked and thus more persuasive. The food servers tested in this vein also received disproportionately higher tips under scientifically controlled experiments where "mirroring" others physically was combined with rephrasing or confirming of their restaurant orders.

As we move forward, it would be a helpful exercise to see if you can identify how these principles are reflected in each of the strategies and skills for handling difficult buyers. With some it may be more obvious than others, but one or more of the RASSCL Principles are always present in the overall skill structure or seller response. Just as in the chapter dealing with introducing benefits where I said using words the buyer uses builds rapport, the concept of "mirroring" is present in various verbal steps in handling buyer attitudes.

Attitudes

Throughout the course of a sales call, as you question to uncover needs, satisfy needs by expanding the benefit, and close the sale, you will inevitably encounter various "attitudes" from the buyer—attitudes that tell you what the buyer is thinking about what you are saying or what you need to be saying.

These attitudes are revealed by things the seller says, or doesn't say, and usually fall into one of five categories:

1.) Cooperation

2.) Skepticism

3.) Indifference

4.) Objection

5.) No relevant response

Number five, of course, isn't an attitude. It's usually an attempt by the buyer to avoid revealing an attitude and requires additional questioning by the seller to discern what attitude is being hidden. If the buyer continues to avoid giving a "relevant" response, a response that tells you what his/her attitude is, then the attitude is usually one of "exaggerated" or "extreme" indifference and stronger action is required. We'll take a look at this stronger action when we deal with Attitude #3 above, "Indifference."

Cooperation

Cooperation is usually evident when you have a buyer that is listening, providing information, and reacting favorably to what you say. Your task is infinitely simpler in these sales calls. Be careful, however, not to confuse friendliness, or a buyer who merely enjoys talking, with one that is ready to part with his or her money.

It's important to avoid wasting time in front of people who are merely friendly or polite, but aren't potential buyers. The questioning techniques discussed in earlier chapters will help insure that this does not happen. My experience revealed time and again that Elite Sellers understand the value of getting to the point and of asking questions of even the most cooperative buyer as a way of delineating politeness from willingness to buy.

In any event, with a cooperative buyer you merely continue to ask general questions, followed by specific questions, and listen for opportunities to introduce a product benefit. Eventually, you close the sale by summarizing those benefits and requesting the appropriate commitment.

Skepticism

The attitude of Skepticism is when the buyer does not believe something you've said. You've questioned the buyer and uncovered needs or problems, and then explained that your product or service can satisfy that need or solve that problem. But, the buyer doesn't believe you. Skepticism is usually not an overriding attitude that defines the entire sales call, but rather one that typically occurs in response to a particular comment or statement that you have made.

In my on-site experience, with insurance agents or software sellers, the attitude of skepticism is often left undiagnosed and therefore not addressed. The chances of closing a sale when the buyer doesn't believe you can provide a benefit he or she considers important are, well…slim at best.

It is important that you develop a good arsenal of data, proof sources, or statements, which can be used to prove important benefits of your product or service. Here's an example:

> Seller: "Mr. Jones, you're right. What good is an insurance policy that can't deliver on its promise after a claim? This is why our agency represents only insurance carriers that are financially able to pay their claims even in the event of a mega-catastrophe like a hurricane."

> Buyer: "That's pretty easy to say, but I know a lot of companies that went belly up after the last hurricane and their agents were probably saying the same thing."

In the two statements above, the seller, an independent insurance agent who represents more than one company has introduced a benefit, that of representing financially stable companies. But, the buyer has expressed doubt or skepticism that it's true. Assuming that the benefit statement was made in response to the buyer expressing the desire for a solvent insurance company, one that can pay its claims, it is important that the skepticism be dealt with... immediately. You do this by making a Proof Statement.

There are three steps to a Proof Statement, as follows:

1.) Restate the benefit.

2.) Offer proof.

3.) Draw the conclusion for the buyer.

Here's how a Proof Statement might sound using the dialogue above.

> Buyer: "That's pretty easy to say, but I know a lot of companies that went belly up after the last hurricane who had agents that were probably saying the same thing."

Restate the benefit: "In this day and age, it's very important that the carrier you buy your business coverage from will be around after the next storm."

Offer Proof: "That's why we represent only companies that are rated A+ by Best's Financial Rating Service. Here, look at this list of our companies and their Best's ratings. You can see they are all among the most financially stable carriers in the United States."

Draw the Conclusion: "So you see, Mr. Jones, not only will you have the best coverage, you'll also have the peace of mind knowing that it will be there no matter how many storms we have next hurricane season."

Now, it's impossible, of course, to know everything that a buyer will be skeptical about. And, you can't always bring your entire set of files, proof sources, testimonials, and the like with you on each sales call. But, it's recommended that you develop some "hard copy" proof sources for the typical and important benefits that buyers may be skeptical about. If you sell insurance in Florida, being able to prove that the company can pay its claims after a mega storm is not asking too much. If you sell software, your companies reputation for upgrades, on-site service and response time are typical issues a buyer might consider important and could question or be skeptical about.

Whatever your industry, spend time developing proof sources for the common benefits that generate skepticism. It's not always a financial record like our example. Sometimes it's a testimonial or letters of recommendation from other buyers about your service or performance. Other times, it can be merely a restatement of facts unknown to the buyer that remove the doubt.

Social Proof
Skepticism is where RASSCL Principle #4, that of Social Proof, often comes into play. It is natural, for example, for Americans to be skeptical about a new luxury car imported from a foreign country. In

1989, midlevel luxury autos, Toyota, Lexus, and the Nissan Infiniti, were first introduced in the US. Their research confirmed the value of Social Proof, so despite being independent competitors they each arrived at the same marketing goal: to be in J.D. Powers' top ten ranking for customer satisfaction. J.D. Powers and Associates rates new cars based on owner satisfaction over varying periods—one month, two months, up to a year—after the purchase. By focusing on follow up communication with their customers, satisfaction surveys, and other post-sale techniques, by 1992, just three years after their debut, all three automobiles were in J.D. Powers' top ten.

Social Proof is so important many Elite Sellers develop a "Proof Source" file and place articles, news ads, letters, testimonials, interoffice memos, and more in it. On important sales calls they take the entire file along, just in case. Some will divide proof sources into different subject categories based on service, financial issues, hardware vs. software problems, etc. I know some old timers in the insurance business who have huge files of this nature and who often find themselves besieged by younger producers looking for something, anything, they can use to prove this, that, or the other point they may have made, but were unable to prove during a previous sales call. Some agencies or businesses maintain office-wide files of this nature so every seller can have access.

Depending on the product or service you offer, the Internet can help provide ready on-site access to proof sources. Some businesses can provide important sales tools, including behavioral studies showing what other buyers are doing, testimonials and the like, via laptops in the hands of talented sellers in the field.

As was often the case, my Elite Sellers were often instinctively using the RASSCL Principles. They knew intuitively that buyers, for certain benefits or features, were not going to take someone's word for it. They knew that without handling the Skepticism by offering some type of proof a seller is likely wasting time attempting to close the sale. Of course, the RASSCL Principle #4 isn't about proving what you say necessarily; it's about being more persuasive by showing customers that other people are behaving a certain way (buying your product or service, for example). This is why testimonials are so important to gather, to keep, and to use.

It is not uncommon for Skepticism to be uncovered after an attempt to close the sale. Maybe the seller wasn't listening for subtle clues indicating that the buyer didn't believe an important benefit of the product or service when it was explained. Maybe, when forced to decide between saying "yes" or saying "no," the buyer merely retreated to Skepticism as a way to avoid parting with his or her money. Either way, you must find out the source of the Skepticism and make a proof statement in order to close the sale. Be prepared!

"Key" Questions

Before we talk about the two most difficult customer attitudes, it's appropriate to mention them in a larger context. Indifference and objection are buyer attitudes that challenge sellers the most and thus are the ones that distinguish successful sellers from those who are not as successful. Spending time becoming proficient with these buyer attitudes, therefore, is paramount to Elite Status.

How wealthy would you be if you were so successful at selling, you were legendary? Not just the best at selling your product, but the best at selling anything; the best in the world. Ben Feldman was such a legend and was so good at selling life insurance he was listed in the *Guinness Book of Records* as the greatest salesman in the world. In most years, he would sell more than $100 million of "individual" life insurance. I talk a little more about Feldman, his sales records, and his approach in the next unit, particularly his penchant for simplicity. Here it's important to mention that his success was based on his proficiency at handling the attitudes of indifference and objection.

Feldman had two particularly helpful talents. The first was his skill at "finding the key" to a prospects problem by using life insurance and other financial planning instruments. His second skill was his use of penetrating questions to bring that concept to the buyer's attention, particularly buyers voicing difficult objections about price or other product drawbacks. Once, for example, when a prospect was expressing indifference, perhaps "extreme indifference," to a personal life insurance policy, Feldman paused and said, "May I ask you one question. Will your widow dress as well as your wife does?" To which the prospect, who had theretofore taken over the conversation, immediately responded "What do you mean?" thus giving control back to Feldman.

The point is, as we look at ways to handle difficult buyers, those who have the attitudes of indifference or objection, particularly objections difficult to overcome, it's important to be prepared with both offsetting benefits of your product or service as well as probing questions to introduce those benefits. Feldman could've just said, "With a life insurance policy, you can be sure your wife will continue to dress well after you die." But…how she was going dress wasn't the point. By using a question, one that startles or that is subtle in its meaning and with an obscure answer, you can often gain control over a difficult buyer or selling situation. This is because you are suddenly the only person in the world who can give the buyer what he/she is dying to have…an answer!

Begin now, today, thinking of questions that can help you get a tighter hold of a recalcitrant buyer. Make a list. Practice applying them to a number of different benefits or features. Start with the most common objections. Then think of the most compelling benefits you can introduce to handle indifference. Run the list by others to gain their input and comments. These are the tools that distinguish an Elite Seller from the rest of the pack. Keep them in mind as we discuss the steps in handling indifference and objection.

Indifference
Indifference is when the buyer sees no need for your product or no need to make a change from his/her current product. You must, therefore, create the need, draw on the "key questions," and closely control the conversation in order to direct the customer to areas where he/she might reveal, or at least reluctantly admit to having, needs or problems.

This attitude may be the most difficult to handle, even more difficult than objection. While you should begin the sales call with general questions, when you don't receive meaningful responses and diagnose the customer as being indifferent, you must move to questions that are more specific to force the customer to respond with a statement of need. Usually indifference requires specific questions, question statements, or general benefit statements because the buyer is giving you no information, good or bad. With an objection, you at least know what the problem is so you can clear it up or minimize it. With indifference, there is no problem but, there is no interest and you must, therefore, create it.

Often the techniques covered under the title "Directing the Sales Call" are helpful, as are the key questions you may have developed—either of which can be necessary in dealing with an indifferent customer.

Extreme Indifference
Sometimes an indifferent buyer is extremely indifferent and may respond to your general benefit statements with things like: "That's nice" or "interesting." Sometimes they say nothing at all and your attempts to open them up repeatedly fail.

I recall a sales presentation I heard as the vice president of Marketing for Shamrock Automation Systems. The seller's name was Lee Pearce and he had been called in to explain an incentive program for the 15 account execs I had hired and trained and who were now operating from their homes in other states. Basically, his product provided an all expense paid trip (and other benefits) to the most productive sellers within designated time frames.

His company provided all the brochures, materials, and motivational information. Sellers who met or exceeded certain sales thresholds then became eligible for a trip to Jamaica, all expenses paid. If they truly excelled and were the top producer they got a cash bonus from the company, and, of course, my undying gratitude. Frankly, product development was behind, sales were lagging, and I thought an incentive bonus program might give the company a needed year-end boost in revenue.

Nonetheless, Mr. Pearce was delivering the first in a series of pre-sentations I had scheduled from various other sellers of incentive programs. This meant that my job was to not buy from Mr. Pearce, not on this day, but to wait until I heard more presentations. Mr. Pearce's job, on the other hand, was to get a commitment from me during this meeting and freeze out the competition that had the benefit of presenting "after" he did. But, his sales approach revealed the danger of relying exclusively on only one RASSCL Principle, in this case Principle #5—Consistency.

Pearce had a table top flip chart, which he placed on the conference room credenza. He flipped a page. Then, he read aloud the various facts about his company and how his incentive program was im-proving sales figures all over America. Then he flipped to another page or chart. Each chart was colorful and informative. Some were humorous; a few had pictures of sunbathers relaxing poolside or on the beach, enjoying their free vacation after having propelled their company to new heights of production.

Pearce's pattern became painfully obvious. He ended each series of charts and fact statement with a question to me along the lines of "wouldn't you agree with that?" Then, another set of facts and, again, "and, wouldn't you agree with that, Mr. Johnson?" Of course I knew, as would most buyers, that answering "yes" to Mr. Pearce would lead inexorably to the final conclusion which, if I disagreed, would mean that I had been lying when I answered all his previous questions with a "yes." It would've meant I had been "inconsis-tent." I felt certain his final question would be something along the lines of, "therefore, wouldn't you have to agree our incentive plan is just what you need to buy, TODAY?"

Anticipating his obvious end game and having a contrary goal, I played it cool, barely responding to his questions and thus preserv-ing my ability to say "no" and not be inconsistent with earlier posi-tions—extreme indifference. I wanted to have an out, so I avoided saying anything that would sound like a firm commitment. When directly pushed for an answer, I used phrases like "I suppose so," "if you say so," "sure, why not?" or "guess so."

Pearce had nothing from which to formulate a benefit statement or with which to direct his sales call—assuming he was listening instead of focusing on his charts and reciting his "canned" presentation.

Buyers who behave as I did with Mr. Pearce are said to have the attitude of extreme indifference. That is, they aren't responding with anything relevant and the questions you ask, the benefits you talk about, nothing seems to make a difference.

They fall into category number five above and have "no relevant response " with which you can introduce a benefit, ask a specific question, or even carry on much of a conversation. As in the game of tennis, you have to develop your own pace whenever your opponent isn't hitting the ball hard enough. Again, the techniques covered under "Directing the Sales Call" are helpful with this particular type of customer attitude. So is proficiency at asking Key Questions as Ben Feldman was adept at doing.

Poor Mr. Pearce was completely unprepared to do so. Or, at least he acted as though he was by just continuing with his canned presentation, as he had been coached and as he had practiced probably dozens of times. He never stopped to ask me a question, a "key" question or any question, that I could respond to with information about my needs, problems, or concerns. Just like the game of tennis, Extreme Indifference requires more skill and can often lead to frustration and an early departure. It shouldn't!

The Trial Close
In these situations, when you encounter extreme indifference, it's appropriate, indeed mandatory to attempt to close the sale. That's right...close the sale! Summarize the benefits you've attempted to introduce, give the customer a choice, and assume the sale has been made, then...ASK FOR THE ORDER!

At first, even sellers with extremely high Ego Drive will have a hard time accepting this as a rational approach. But, think about it. What's the buyer's reaction going to be? Won't it have to be something along the lines of the following?

"Now, wait just a minute! I never said I wanted to buy your product! I've got a lot of problems with this concept. You haven't answered a single one of my concerns!!"

That's certainly what I said to Mr. Pearce, when, as illogical as it was, he finished his script by asking me to cut a check.

Unfortunately Pearce was not an Elite Seller. He didn't know about Indifference. He didn't know about closing a sale as a way to open up a customer. He didn't know about the Principles of Persuasion, RASSCL Principle #5—Commitment/Consistency, or Reciprocation, or Social Proof, or Scarcity, or how to foster the Liking Principle with general questions and benefit statements. He just packed up his easel and said that if I changed my mind I should call him. I couldn't believe it! He was someone who sold a product allegedly designed to motivate sellers, but he missed the basics of selling by a wide margin.

The Elite Seller, one who was listening instead of talking, one who was prepared to uncover needs, one who begins with general questions, and one who was truly trying to uncover customer needs would have responded to my statement "You haven't answered a single one of my concerns!!" by simply asking...

"Can you tell me what some of those concerns are?"

In other words, the closing works similar to one of Feldman's key questions. The unresponsive, extremely indifferent customer is forced to give you information, important sales information. They want to appear logical and consistent (RASSCL #5), so they must now tell you why they don't want to buy. Perhaps they will tell you about a need or problem they have. Perhaps they'll reveal an objection, which you will handle. Perhaps they are skeptical, in which case you'll offer proof. Whatever their attitude or problem, you now have the buyer's attention and can begin the sales process.

This is sometimes referred to as a "Trial Close" by other teachers. I've even heard a few say that it can be used at the beginning of every sales call as a way to "take charge" or to "get the buyer's attention." Frankly, if you read the prologue, those who believe that or who operate this way are likely the old school sellers in my opinion. Never assume the customer will or won't do anything. Find out and respond accordingly, using the skills of today's Elite Sellers. If you encounter extreme indifference, make a closing statement. It just might work.

Objection

Objection is the attitude often thought of as being the most difficult to handle. Other than extreme indifference, I'm not sure I disagree with that assessment, depending on what type of objection is voiced.

An objection is merely strong opposition to or disagreement with a feature, or lack of a feature, of your product or service. Often, for example, price is an objection, however, not always, depending on the competition's price or the value that accompanies the price.

In literally hundreds of discussion group sessions, the sellers who worked for me began to create a digest of objections they encountered to the product we were all trying to sell across the US. Once we got past the point of distinguishing between a mere question about a feature (or lack of a benefit) from an objection about a feature (or lack of a benefit), we were able to begin classifying objections and in so doing develop the optimum seller approach for handling each type. We found some objections to be, well "easy" to handle. And others...not so easy or "difficult" to handle. It's for this reason that we divide objections into two categories, either those based on an "incorrect assumption" or those that are "perceived drawbacks." Either one is a reason the buyer expresses for not buying your product or service.

Incorrect Assumptions (easy objections) are objections that incorrectly assumed something about your product. They are usually based on incorrect information or rumors or misinterpretations of something the buyer read, deduced, heard, or...assumed.

One way to describe Incorrect Assumptions is to say this type of objection is simply wrong or based on "incorrect" information. The buyer objects to your software system because it doesn't have remote dial in capabilities, when, in fact, it does have such capabilities. Or, the buyer doesn't want to buy a homeowners insurance policy from your agency or company because it doesn't have protection for a rather extensive jewelry and fur collection, when such coverage is offered by endorsement to the main policy.

With an Incorrect Assumption the buyer objects because your product or service lacks something that he or she believes is important for it to have or it has a feature that he or she objects to. Either way, because the buyer's objection is based on incorrect or limited information and thus is often referred to as an "easy" objection, inexperienced sellers often squander the opportunity by merely blurting out their disagreement. Keep reading.

Perceived Drawbacks (difficult objections) are objections based on accurate information in the description of a product feature or lack of a desired feature or benefit. Price often falls into this category of objection.

The easiest way to describe Perceived Drawbacks is to say that the buyer is technically correct in his/her assessment. That is, the feature they object to is present in your product essentially as they understand it, or the one they wish it had isn't available. Price is often a Perceived Drawback but, not always.

Applying the examples of Incorrect Assumptions to define Perceived Drawbacks, we could simply say that the software system mentioned earlier doesn't have remote dial in capabilities or the homeowners' policy your agency sells doesn't provide an endorsement for jewelry and furs. It's because of the innate nature of the Perceived Drawback that such objections are often referred to as difficult to handle.

Handling Objections
Because each requires a dramatically different approach of the seller, let's look at an example or two to make sure you understand the difference between the two types of objections.

Logic should tell you one thing about objections; they must be handled immediately. You cannot let them fester or delay your response with "We'll get to that in a minute." Remember, an objection is a reason *not to buy* and there is no point going on to other benefits if you can't handle the objection that will keep the customer from buying. You must handle an objection immediately.

Make Objections Easier
But first, there are two basic mistakes sellers often make, depending on the type of objection. With the objection based on an Incorrect Assumption, you must avoid sounding like you are correcting the buyer by simply telling the buyer he/she is wrong, or creating that impression. You want to make it easy for them to accept the new information that corrects their "incorrect" assumption.

On the other hand, with a Perceived Drawback, you may have the tendency to overreact with RASSCL Principle #6—Liking, that is, people buy from people they like. In other words, you must avoid "agreeing" with the customer and, in so doing, reinforcing the contention that the existence of the drawback is a legitimate reason not to buy. For example, if a buyer says, "Wow, that's expensive!" You should never respond with "It is expensive, but…"—a natural, but very damaging response.

The steps for handling each type of objection are designed to help you avoid making these mistakes and to maximize the likelihood that the customer will accept your product's benefits, whether the buyer incorrectly assumed something or incorrectly perceived something as a drawback.

Steps to Handling Objections

As with other skills consistent with the RASSCL Principles, there are two steps to handling objections, as follows:

For Incorrect Assumptions:

1.) Expand the objection by rephrasing it in question form; and,

2.) Handle it immediately, offering proof if necessary.

For Perceived Drawbacks:

1.) Minimize the objection by rephrasing it in question form; and,

2.) Use specific questions to lead the customer to benefits (either old ones or new ones not yet introduced) that offset the Perceived Drawback.

Let's talk about the two concepts that underlie the first step in both types of objections. First, you'll notice that regardless of the objection, either easy or difficult, the first step concludes by converting the buyer's statement into "the form of a question." Keep that in mind as we move ahead.

False Objections

For a variety of reasons buyers often give what can be called "false" objections or objections based on matters not related to what they've actually said. Of course, you've got to find out the "real" objection and simply continuing to talk or to assume you've got the objection correctly will rarely do the trick. Here's an example.

A local property and casualty insurance agent is attempting to secure a policy for a small business owner. His client, who is a friend and neighbor, voices an objection that he only does business with A+ financially-rated insurers. The seller's insurance company is not A+ rated.

"XYZ isn't rated A+, is it?" the buyer challenges?

"No, but it is only four years old and capitalized better than many A+ rated carriers," says the seller, unable to resist the contradicting sound of his comment and, in doing so, failing to rephrase the objection in the form of a question.

"Still, you're not A+ rated are you?" the persistent buyer asks again, even more confident he's pinned the seller in a corner.

Unknown to the seller, insurance broker is the "real" objection, and that his friend's father-in-law has just started working in an insurance agency himself and he feels an obligation to buy from him. The buyer didn't want to hurt the seller's (his friend) feelings and he's a bit embarrassed he's let the call go on this long without telling him so.

Similar objections, false objections, occur quite frequently in selling. A buyer, for example, might not know a lot about your company or firm, but doesn't want to offend you by suggesting that it may be too small or untested. So, he merely says something like, "I'd like to sleep on it" or "Let me think about it and I'll call you."

You might have numerous reasons why he should act now, not the least of which is that his current policy is expiring soon and he doesn't want to go without coverage for even a short period of time, but...it won't make any difference if his real objection isn't uncovered.

Perhaps the best way to recognize a false objection is to observe their responses to solid answers. In the example above, the financial rating agency may not even grant A+ rating to companies that haven't been in business more than five years. In other words, what he is asking for is impossible, yet the state regulatory agency has certified your company as financially sound and you have numerous examples of previously A+ rated companies that went out of business or that later became B+ rated. And to top it off, this customer is currently with a company that is rated C+. In other words, their lack of acceptance of your company's financial soundness is not logical and is therefore a "clue" that their real objection is something other than the stated one.

Sometimes a buyer will throw out a series of seemingly unrelated objections that appear to have no basis for the product you are selling or for your firm or company. Eventually, you are faced with a decision. "Is this guy for real?" or "Is he hiding something?" Either way, what have you got to lose by finding out?

> "Mr. Buyer, this software system is recognized as the best in its class. It has the best service record in the marketplace. It has the online features you wanted and said were important. So, I've got to ask you, "What's really on your mind here?"

> "Well, to tell you the truth..." — and they come right out with it. And, if they don't come out with it, what have you lost by using this approach?

Anyway, this is one of the reasons why it's important to rephrase objections, all objections, in the form of a question.

Next, notice that with objections based on Incorrect Assumptions step one is to expand the objection by rephrasing it in the form of a question. What does "expand the objection" mean and why do we want to do it?

In this context, the word "expand" means to increase its importance or to make it seem bigger or more relevant than it might otherwise appear to be. The reason for doing this is that you are going to clear it up in the next step and, in so doing, eliminate the reason the buyer was saying he/she was not going to buy your product or service. By way of example, and using the products above, we could rephrase by saying something like:

> "So, if I understand you correctly, you're saying that your biggest problem and a major reason you're reluctant to buy ACME Software is that there's no remote dial in capabilities?"

Then, assuming you're right and the customer acknowledges that fact, you can clear up the objection based on an Incorrect Assumption by simply saying something like:

"First, you're right to be concerned about the remote dial in function. It's a must these days. But, you can rest easy because ACME has its own proprietary dial in system recognized as the most sophisticated in the business. Here, take a look at this brochure which has several quotes from satisfied customers. You can see that with this dial in system you'll get all the benefits you're after."

What was achieved here is that the buyer is expressing an increased value in a benefit your product provides by agreeing with your rephrasing (and expansion) of their objection. In other words, the value of the benefit is expanded and appears more important, which means that when you solve their problem your solution is more important—thus you've moved dramatically closer to making a closing statement. Keep in mind, this is contrasted with the natural response along the lines of, "No, you're wrong…we do have a dial up system."

Can you see why some people say that objections are good things to encounter because they give sellers information leading to a close? And, in the case of an Incorrect Assumption, they often result in strong buying signals from the buyer?

On the other hand, the first step in handling an objection due to a Perceived Drawback is to minimize it, again, by rephrasing it in the form of a question. In other words you want to do the opposite of what was done with the Incorrect Assumption, which was to expand the objection. Here you want to make it seem smaller and thus surmountable and you want to lead right into the offsetting benefits.

In general, there are several reasons to rephrase an objection. One, it buys a little time, which can be important if you've been caught off guard or this is the first time you've uncovered this objection. Two, it clarifies the objection, which is important and the lack of which is an often overlooked reason for an unsuccessful close. It also helps you learn whether it may be a false objection. And three, it shows you are listening and that the buyer's objection, whether incorrect or false or a Perceived Drawback, is important to you. Finally, rephrasing the objection in the form of a question helps to keep you from "agreeing" with it. Keep reading!

How many times, in response to the buyer saying, "Boy, that's expensive," have you said something that begins with...

"It is expensive, but..."?

If you're honest, your answer may be that you do it every time. Frankly, whether something is expensive is quite a relative matter. Cost has no meaning unless it's compared to the benefits of the purchase. An old desktop computer may be expensive if it costs $5,000. A Cadillac Escalade, on the other hand, would be considered quite inexpensive at the same price. Your job is to make the desktop computer appear more like the Escalade.

Of course, that may not always be possible. It may be that your customer wants something your product doesn't have. Therefore you probably know ahead of time what that is. In fact, it should be part of your usual sales portfolio or your company or industry training. You know and therefore should be prepared to offer benefits that offset that Perceived Drawback.

And that brings us to step two in handling an objection created by a Perceived Drawback: use specific questions to lead the customer to benefits (either old ones or new ones not yet introduced) that offset the Perceived Drawback.

It's basically the process the Elite Seller has employed throughout the entire sales call, but placed in the context of one objection raised by the buyer. After you rephrase in the form of a question, you may start with a line of questions and the conversation could go something like this:

Buyer: I'm sorry but $8,000 is far more than I can spend on a homeowners policy.

Seller: So, you're saying that price is your primary concern here?

Buyer: Well, yes. Frankly, I don't have that kind of money just lying around, 'ya know."

Seller: Well, let me ask you this. Didn't we agree that protection for your coin collection was important and that you may not have had that adequately covered under your existing policy?

Buyer: Well, yes, I suppose we did but I don't know.

Seller's Specific Benefit Statement: Exactly right. We did agree on that because your coin collection is important to you and losing it, permanently, with no reimbursement would be a devastating loss.

Seller: And, what about the fact that every other agent you talked to said their company wouldn't provide liability protection if your pit bull were to bite or injure someone. Doesn't that have some value above the usual price consideration?

Buyer: I suppose.

Seller's Specific Benefit Statement: Of course it does. You don't want to give up your pet and XYZ doesn't believe you ought to have to either.

Seller: Mr. Jones, the fact is cheaper insurance isn't always the best deal. What good is it if it isn't customized for your specific exposures?

Buyer: Well, I can see your point. But, I don't know if it's worth $8,000.

Seller: Well, let me ask you this then. Your home would cost about $1.2 million to rebuild, right?

Buyer: Yes.

Seller: That's a major asset, maybe the most valuable one you've ever owned. What would happen to you if it were destroyed by a hurricane and the company that insured it wasn't financially sound enough to pay your claim along with everybody else's?

Buyer: That wouldn't be good. I'd be calling you to find out why.

Seller: Exactly my point. If you buy from XYZ Company with its A+ rating, you won't have to call me because your claim will be paid, hassle free. With catastrophic losses so prevalent nowadays, there's great value in having the piece of mind to know that your company will be there for you when the wind blows.

Buyer: Of course, I agree. Remember, my previous carrier went bankrupt after the 2004 storms and I was just lucky that my claim was under the State Guaranty Fund limit. I don't know what I would've done if it had been a total loss.

Seller: I'm afraid you would've had to spend your own money, probably more than $1.2 million to rebuild your home. Wouldn't paying an $8,000 premium have been worth avoiding that?

Buyer: Yes, of course it would.

Obviously, at this point, the buyer has come full circle. With your help, they now realize that saving money on insurance can be like sleeping in the park to save on rent. Their most valued assets—their home, their pet, their coin collection, their life—is certainly worth $8,000. And, because you rephrased the objection, you never acquiesced or said that $8,000 was a lot of money. In fact, the Escalade' parked in your clients driveway costs more than five times that amount and all it does is depreciate.

HANDLING OBJECTIONS

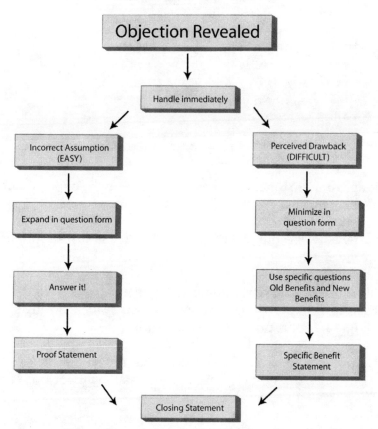

The Ledger Approach

History credits Benjamin Franklin for coming up with something called the "T" approach. It can be used in closing a sale or in handling an objection that stems from a Perceived Drawback while being consistent with the RASSCL Principles, particularly #5—Consistency/Commitment.

After drawing a large "T" across a piece of paper and labeling each side as either pluses or minuses (similar to an accounting ledger), you proceed to question the buyer and make Specific Benefit Statements as in our example above. Then, you fill in the ledger as you go.

Perceived Drawback (Difficult Objections)
Benjamin Franklin "Ledger" Approach

Pluses	Minuses
-Complete Protection for Valuable Coin Collection	-Slightly Higher Premium
-Dangerous Breed Dog Bite Coverage for Lawsuits	
-Soluency Protection with A Rated Carrier	
-Full Insurance to Value of $1.2 million	
-All the Other Provisions of Competitors Policy	
-"Peace of Mind"	

At the appropriate time, you can pause, hold up the paper, point to it, and ask, "It doesn't look like it adds up does it?" or…

"Now, what was your concern again?" or "and your problem was…" etc.

Frankly, since having just summarized all the benefits, as in this example, and with each of them so visibly displayed, a closing statement might be appropriate. You could simply say…

"You know, looking at this ledger I'd say the only question is to ask how you want to pay the premium, in installments or one lump sum?"

An Important Summary
You now have all the strategies for handling all the Seller Attitudes, as follows:

Platform I—Selling Skills

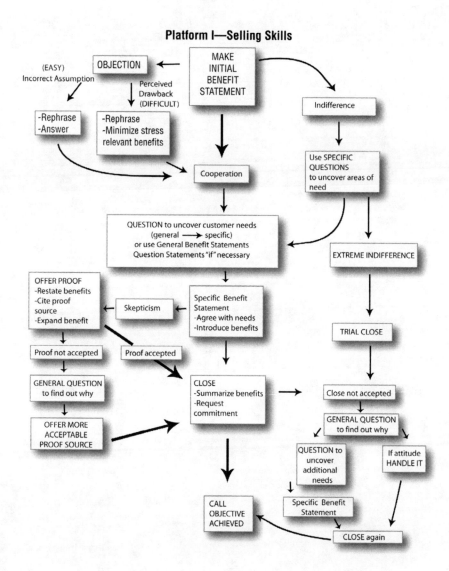

Chapter 13

INTANGIBLE SELLING

It's impossible for something you can't see, touch, or smell to look, feel, or smell bad...sj

One of the things I used to hear a lot from insurance sellers and those who sold financial products was that their selling was more difficult than "normal" selling because an intangible product was somehow more difficult to sell. I don't agree—different, perhaps, but not inherently more difficult.

I say this because "intangibility" means that a product doesn't have the drawbacks of a tangible product either. Insurance doesn't smell bad. Class II bonds don't have an unattractive appearance. Annuities can't look too small for their intended space and rarely possess any of the physical shortcomings typical of tangible products like cars, computers, or real estate. Insurance, securities, service contracts, and the like may be intangible, but...intangibility isn't what makes them difficult to sell (assuming they are). It is the seller's inability or failure to recognize and then to capitalize on the difference that is their challenge.

Basic Analogies

The talented Elite Seller often capitalizes on an intangible's lack of physical characteristics by creating pictures in the customer's mind—those that relate to the physical world. By creative use of analogies and other descriptions, it's possible to paint the perfect mental picture in the buyer's mind. This cannot be done so easily with a physical product that can be seen, heard, sniffed, or otherwise detected by the senses, and which does not measure up to the mental picture the customer had of the product he wanted to buy. But, it can be done with intangibles.

One word of caution is that this technique works best when closing the sale or when handling an objection or at least after the seller has enough knowledge and familiarity with the client to know the right analogy to use—or the one or two analogies that should not be used. It's possible to go too far or to choose the wrong analogy, so...use caution and wait until you've developed some familiarity when you're selling to a completely new prospect.

An analogy can be used to clarify an unfamiliar point with a familiar example unrelated to the product. An analogy can help the buyer visualize something that will help him/her understand a technical point about a complicated feature of your product.

At one of my sales meetings, we spent some time identifying analogies that members of the team were using. This helped me in classifying analogies into two types: basic and interactive. The basic analogy is a simple reference to something else (usually something tangible) to describe your product or a feature of your product.

"This policy is as good as gold!"

"This is the Mercedes-Benz of the annuities industry."

"Our company finances are like a Sherman Tank, impenetrable."

"Our service response time is fast as lightning!"

Again, a word of caution; the basic analogy can be overused. A sales call peppered with too many can come across as trite, manufactured, or simply as unprofessional sales hype—not always, not if used judiciously, but sometimes if you're not careful. But, unlike the basic analogies above, the interactive analogy is not so prone to misinterpretation.

Interactive Analogies

The interactive analogy has a twofold purpose: one, to capture your buyer's imagination; and two, to get the buyer to participate in both the analogy and the selling conversation. It works by the seller first describing a simple problem and then asking the buyer for the obvious solution.

In handling a buyer who is procrastinating on making a decision and has said something like, "I know it's good, but I just need to move more slowly on this," an Elite Seller might say:

"Mr. Buyer let me ask you something. If you saw two identical motorcycles, which one are you more likely to look at—the one that's parked or the one doing the wheelie at 50 mph? That's because action attracts attention; it gets things done. It's worth looking at. Let's go ahead and take some action with this proposal. Make something happen with your company's software programs today."

In introducing a benefit or explaining the value of a benefit, an Elite Seller might say:

"Bob, do you know why so many people died on the Titanic?" [Pause long enough to hear him blame it on hitting an iceberg or on freezing water, etc.] And then say...

"Actually that's a common myth; virtually everyone would have lived if the Titanic simply had enough life boats. And, that's my point; you see, buying this plan (policy, proposal, feature, etc.) is like traveling on an ocean liner. It costs less to own and operate a ship with too few lifeboats, and chances are that you'll never need them. But wouldn't you feel safer traveling on a ship that offered the extra security? Would you ever want to travel on a ship that you knew didn't have enough lifeboats? Me either!

Now, I admit that the extra security you get from our plan may not be needed everyday, but…when it is needed, you'll have the peace of mind knowing it's there."

In overcoming an objection about price or a large initial investment, like with an annuity or a real estate purchase or an insurance premium, divide the cost into small increments. An Elite Seller breaks a $5,200 premium down to $100 per week multiplied by 52 weeks in a year and says something along the lines of:

"Mr. Smith, let me make an analogy. Assume that I came to you and said I'd work for only $100 a week for an entire year and guarantee you a profit over my entire salary and "every" related employment expense. All things being equal, you'd hire me, wouldn't you?"

"You'd hire me even though I need to be paid $5,200 up front for one year because the results are guaranteed. There's no overtime to pay for the extra work on weekends or late nights, and, in addition to the insurance coverage you're getting, I'm going to employ a competent staff at no extra cost to you."

In response to an objection due to a Perceived Drawback an Elite Seller can set the stage for introducing benefits that offset that drawback by using the following analogy:

"Mrs. Williams, what do you see when you look at an iceberg? You really only see the tip right? Well, your concern here is really just the tip of our product and I'd like you to examine the other two-thirds lying beneath the surface. So, let me ask you a few questions…" etc.

You can see by the examples that use of analogies can be quite helpful when selling an intangible product. Frankly, depending on the situation, analogies can be helpful anytime the customer is having difficulty visualizing the benefit or is questioning the value of a particular feature.

As always, any one of the above statements could be used for a wide variety of products or services. They may not fit exactly to your product and certainly not to every situation. The point is that every skill in this book is subject to adaptation and habit. Use the examples or sample phrases described herein as guides. Take the analogies above and adapt them to fit your product or service. Write them out. Practice saying them in a wide variety of situations. Begin doing this now, early in your career, and later they'll be a habitual part of your Elite Seller's repertoire.

Begin building the habit!

Chapter 14

PRICE & PROCRASTINATION
At some point, the quality of one's decision isn't nearly as important as the need for one to be made...sj

I found that regardless of an Elite Seller's proficiency using the skills in the opening chapters, it is often difficult to overcome two particular buyer reactions. I call them the dynamic duo of buyer avoidance: Price and Procrastination. Either one can be so easily thrown up as the ultimate buyer defense shield.

With Price, the buyer can say:

> "It's too much right now."

> "It's not in the budget."

> "I simply don't have the money."

With Procrastination, the buyer can say:

> "I just want to wait."

> "Let me think it over."

> "Let me talk with our CFO first."

In each instance above, the avoidance is not related to your product but to an internal and seemingly insurmountable issue of the buyer or his/her company.

Helping buyers is your job as an Elite Seller. You must be prepared to help them not only buy your product, assuming that was the goal of the sales call, but help them buy it today.

Preparation for Procrastination
Every sales call occupies a unique place in the overall selling cycle. With some products you must meet with the buyer many times. With some products you must deal with others before you meet with the decision maker who will make a decision based on the recommendation of the others you have already met with.

To help with Procrastination, whenever appropriate you should request that all decision makers be present at the sales presentation. Depending on the product or stage of the sales cycle, a partner, manager, accountant, or spouse may need to be present. Be up front with prospects and say you expect them to be able to make a decision after you have presented all the facts. It's not unusual for an Elite Seller to say, prior to making a presentation and right after preliminary small talk:

> "I enjoyed that chat and I always appreciate being able to talk candidly with someone who has the ability to make a decision on an important matter like this."

In other words, the Elite Seller set the buyer up to know he/she expected a decision and expected it from this buyer. The Elite Seller put the buyer in the mindset to behave as a decision maker by making the decision.

Sometimes it may be necessary to share with a buyer the fact that some people actually meet with you and don't have enough guts to tell you they cannot make a decision. At the end of the presentation, this puts your current prospect in the embarrassing position of having to tell you they are one of those inconsiderate people. I've accompanied Elite Sellers on calls when they've said to an executive:

"Now, before I begin, you are the person I should be talking to, right?" Then, they might even add something like, "Am I to understand you have the authority to make a yes or no decision today?" Even selling encyclopedias door to door, this would be important.

My top seller for the state of Pennsylvania would often use the following:

"Can we agree on something? I'm not going to waste your time with high-pressure sales techniques; I'm just going to show you the best automated rating system money can buy. All I'll do is prove how good it is and let you decide whether you want to buy it. In return for that, I would only ask that if you agree it's what I say it is that you'll buy it today and not make me come back later. Does that sound fair?"

Often, you'll meet with someone who is to present a recommendation to the decision maker, but who tells you the boss will go along with his/her recommendation and has delegated both the responsibility and the authority to your buyer for making the right recommendation. In these instances, be sure to find out if there are any guiding principles or parameters set for the recommendation. That is, find out what you need to know in order to present a proposal that will meet the boss' criteria.

The Scarcity Principle

Every year, one line of automobile outsells all the others. Sometimes the same car will lead the pack for several years in a row only to be replaced by someone else down the road. But, for too long prior to 2003, one automobile was consistently at the bottom of the national sales charts. Nothing, it seemed, could revive its slumping sales. Even advertising was avoided because it was so in the red the company couldn't afford any. Then, suddenly in 2003, without making any engineering or design changes, without offering any special pricing or doing any marketing, the same company outsold every other auto manufacturer, domestic and foreign, and did so by a dramatic margin. In fact, it exceeded all US sales projections, both its own and those of the most trusted economic prognosticators.

Who was the car company? It was Oldsmobile. Why did it suddenly outsell all the others? GM had announced that 2003 would be the last year it would manufacture and sell its Oldsmobile line.

That same year, the world's only supersonic passenger jet, the Concorde, announced it would terminate service at a date certain, also due to lack of sales. Suddenly, all of its seats were booked solid; despite price increases, and by individuals who had previously not seen fit to fly on the Concorde.

Under what was dubbed the "marketing fiasco of the decade," Coca Cola announced it was changing the formula of the worlds most popular soft drink, Coke, in favor of New Coke. It did so after exhaustive taste testing that conclusively demonstrated people preferred the taste of New Coke.

But...the backlash was unprecedented. Coke lovers everywhere rose up. They organized to bring "traditional" coke back. This was all despite the fact that many had been involved in blind taste tests having indicated they preferred the taste of "New" Coke. Still they fought with everything they had. They filed legal challenges; established a hotline that quickly got 60,000 calls; T-shirts were sold; PR and advertising campaigns were set in play to bring back traditional Coke. All this despite a clear preference for New Coke of 55 percent to 45 percent.

Unfortunately, in Coca Cola's taste tests, the brand that wasn't available at the time, was New Coke. And so, in keeping with the Scarcity Principle, it was the preferred taste. That is until it became known that old Coke was going away...then it was preferred with a passion that eventually caused the demise of New Coke altogether. RASSCL Principle #3—Scarcity, was determining options more than taste. In the end, what was left for everyone to ponder was whether Coca Cola had actually been guilty of committing the marketing fiasco of the decade or one of the most daringly brilliant promotional moves of all time.

The list goes on and on. Details of the Scarcity Principle may differ, not only from product to product, or industry to industry, but from one buyer to another, but…it works! The point is to keep the Scarcity Principle in mind during your sales call and particularly at the time of your closing. You must build a sense of urgency into the sale by having a reason(s) for the buyer to buy now, from you. The price, the product, the options—something is going away and by waiting the buyer will only run the risk of losing the opportunity to have that something.

Thinking It Over
Probably the most common way buyers circumvent having to buy from someone who's done a good job explaining all the real benefits of a product and overcoming all objections, misunderstandings, Perceived Drawbacks, or false objections, is to say "I'd like to think it over."

It's tough to treat this as a traditional objection, rephrasing in the form of a question: "So, if I understand you correctly, you're saying that the reason you don't want to buy right now is that you'd like to think it over?" It doesn't really make sense for two rational human beings to be clarifying something so obviously stated.

Because Procrastination is typical of so many people, especially when doing something painful like spending money, if you are not prepared you will lose many, many sales. Unfortunately, there aren't any "pat" answers guaranteed to work on every buyer. A lot depends on how things have gone in the call up to the point the buyer said he/she would like to think it over. A lot depends on the product and how timely your offer is. Insurance may need to be purchased or may be required by a mortgage lender. A network system may need to be installed on a particular date to avoid any downtime. For our purposes here, suffice it to say that you need to be prepared for those times when you don't have a rational reason for the buyer to buy now, or at least be prepared to make it appear rational.

Remember the seller who worked for me named Jonnie? She was asking too many specific questions about pricing issues in the beginning of her calls and we worked together on a solution. Months later, she became one of my top sellers and I went back to see how she was doing and witnessed her technique for dealing with Procrastination from a husband and wife we called on. In response to her closing statement, they said, "You know, what you've said sounds great, but we'd like to talk it over."

To which Jonnie responded, "You know, you two are just like my husband and me."

"How's that?" the couple replied.

"Well, we like to talk things over, too. So, I want you to take your time, talk it over, and don't feel any pressure from me."

Then, she sat back and waited for them to discuss it. When they paused, a bit confused, she said, "Would you like me to wait in another room? I have some calls I can make."

It was a great technique in that situation. The couple actually said, "No need to leave." Then turning to each other: "So, what do you think honey?"

"I think this is what we're looking for; how about you?"

"Me too!"

And so the sale was closed.

Sometimes in response to "I'd like to think it over," I heard an Elite Seller respond with something like:

"You go right ahead. In the meantime, I'll be in the reception area making a few calls so you can let me know when you're finished."

Of course, the phrase "thinking it over" often means a whole lot more than just a few minutes; but, given ten minutes, an Elite Seller will come back and say something like:

"I have great news! I just called the office and found out we can bind coverage today and finance the premium over twelve months. If we do that, then all I need is one-third of the total today."

Please keep in mind, there is no excuse for entering any selling situation without an arsenal of reasons to "buy today." Optional approaches to paying, to product delivery, to reducing the price, or optional versions of the product, its features, or number of features—everything should always be at the disposal of an Elite Seller who has done his or her homework.

Just like having testimonials as proof that you provide good service, you ought to have a reason for every customer to buy now. Practice it. Repeat it. Try new methods and approaches, but never, never go into a sales call without a plan for overcoming Procrastination.

A seller of life insurance once told me his response to "I'd like to think it over."

"If I put a feather in your pocket without you knowing it, do you think you could tell it was there, if you didn't put your hand in your pocket?"

"I'm sure I wouldn't"

"But, if one by one, I put another feather in your pocket until there was a handful of feathers or enough to stuff a pillow with, you might know they were there wouldn't you?"

"Sure...but, what's your point?"

"Life insurance is the same way. It's something you need and the longer you wait to get it the more it's going to cost. Without you even realizing, it becomes a bigger and bigger burden until, heaven forbid, you become ill or injured and it might not be available to you at all."

"All I'm asking you to do today is buy a feather compared to the price you'll have to pay if you wait. What do you say; would you like the monthly or the semi-annual pay plan?"

This "feather" analogy worked so well, this seller actually began taping a small feather to the last page of his written proposals. When the buyer asked what it was for, the seller had the perfect answer. Sometimes, in the absence of a written proposal, he carried one in his pocket and would place it on the buyer's desk to begin the analogy.

Having the Best Price
Having the best price is always nice. It makes the sale easier and it makes selling almost like, well, it isn't selling, but more like taking orders. But, if price was always the only buyer consideration there would be only one product of each type available. It would be constructed in the least costly way so that it could have the lowest possible price. No one would need any other product options, if they had a higher price, and no one would need to have the benefits (other than price) explained to them. In short, there would be no need for anything to be sold and therefore, no need for sellers.

Most sellers shudder at the price of their product, unless it is the lowest price, in which case they shudder at the quality or the lack of product features they have. Rarely does any one product have it all and when it does, mass marketing is usually the most efficient way to distribute it, not sales people.

One Word of Advice
If you have the best or most competitive price, never mention it. Talk about everything else first. Mention any product feature and expand on it for the buyer. Ask the buyer questions and introduce benefits. But, don't mention the price until they are almost begging you for it.

This works because you have the best price. Why not take all the time you need to expand on other benefits just to make certain that the buyer has all that you have to offer in addition to the best price?

Also, if you sell price, you may encounter a buyer that believes benefits other than price are important and disagreeing with the buyer in your approach may not be wise.

Finally, you may not always have the best price and selling price is something you could live to regret. Insurance or other annualized products are typical examples. What happens when you tell a customer that the price of your policy is low and that's why they should buy from you? Next year, when your price isn't so low, you have, in essence, told the buyer to look for the seller that might now have a price lower than yours.

The Timing of Price
Prospects, particularly if they are business people, often push sellers to discuss the price of their product or service way before they have any idea of what value they might be acquiring for that price. Elite Sellers are skilled at deferring price questions so that they can continue to build value in the buyer's mind before quoting the price.

With some products, there is a sales cycle that involves the possibility of price customization based on different levels of product or the inclusion or deletion of certain features...or the forfeiture of some profit.

Insurance is a good example. Increase the deductible and the price could go down. Lower the limits and the premium could be reduced. Do both and you could save substantial dollars.

But, there's also the element of the need for a survey with many products. That is, surveying to find out what the customers situation is (with insurance, it's called exposures, loss potential, or underwriting) in order to determine insurability and/or price. With insurance or other products, it's possible the survey could be quite lengthy and involve other issues like an appraisal or replacement cost estimate before a price can be determined. Depending on the competition, this could even be helpful to the sales process. However, if you are in the situation where you know the price and it's time to sell the product at that price, here are some techniques for postponing the discussion until the most opportune time:

"Mr. Jones, I am glad you asked me that question. I'll get to it in a minute, but first I need to hear a few things from you."

"Mrs. Greene, it really depends on how you are going to purchase it. I'll figure that for you in a minute, but may I ask you some questions first?"

"It's really important that I know some things in order to calculate a price to value equation for you. May I ask you some questions in order to do that?"

"Bill, let's discuss whether or not you even like this product before we figure how much it will cost you to get it."

"At this point, I could only guess at the price. If you'll give me a few moments, I could come up with something more accurate and meaningful for you."

"Mr. Smith, you're right to be concerned about price, but let me ask if I can follow the old adage of saving the best for last."

Any one of the above statements could be used for a wide variety of products or services. They may not fit exactly to your product and certainly not to every situation. The point is to use them as a guide for developing one or two that fit your product or service. Write them out. Practice saying them in a wide variety of situations. Build the habit!

Another set of phrases utilize the technique of building suspense, as follows:

"Before I explain the price to you, I want you to know that this is the absolute best policy money can buy and it has the best coverage on the marketplace today. Now, would you like to know why I say that?"

"Before I tell you the cost of our network system, I'd like to point out that it contains a new operating system that will reduce your downtime by 30 percent. Did you know about that?"

"Please remember that this policy reflects additional coverage based on appreciation of your building and has a more significant payout in the event of a covered claim. There are three areas where improvements have been made. Would you like to hear them?"

"There are some features here that pay back what you spend over time. Can I tell you about those so that the price can be understood in the appropriate context?"

As always, the point is to use these as a guide for developing one or two that fit your product or service. Write them out. Practice saying them in a wide variety of situations. And, as always, begin building the habit!

Having a Higher Price

Sometimes your price is higher than other similar products. Elite Sellers never apologize for that and maintain a positive attitude about it. Buyers tend to respect this attitude, and, if they sense any regret on your part, they may try to chisel the price down. But, being proud of a higher price and using it as a benefit rather than a drawback is also a legitimate and often successful approach. Dale Carnegie, Zig Ziglar, and other great sellers of our time were known for techniques that exposed the highest price as a sign that the product was better, more noteworthy in the eyes of others, and, in the long run, a better deal.

The most cited expert on persuasion, Robert Cialdini, was once called by a friend of his who owned a jewelry store about a seemingly unbelievable occurrence to which she requested his analysis. She had been trying to sell a new line of turquoise jewelry, but wasn't having any luck. She tried all the usual approaches—moving the display, rearranging the pieces, putting a table outside. Nothing, it seemed, could move even one piece of her turquoise jewelry in this upscale neighborhood.

Before leaving town for three days, in desperation, she clipped a note to her store manager to the display case which said, "Everything on this display 1/2 X price." When she returned three days later, every item of turquoise jewelry was sold. Gone in three days was that which would not sell for three months. How?

She immediately went to the store manager and to her shock found out that her note had been misread. The manager thought she had asked to raise the price by two times (X), not cut it in half. In other words, the manager had doubled the price and, because she did, people thought the jewelry was worth more and thus worthy of being purchased. Cialdini explained to his friend that when someone has no particular expertise about a product they must rely on others or on other facts. Price, in this instance, was what these upscale buyers used to determine whether or not an unfamiliar line of jewelry, about which they knew very little, was worthy of being purchased. I mentioned earlier that it is not a good idea to agree with the customer's objection about price by saying something like, "Yes, it is expensive but…". This shows that, in the discretion of the seller, there may be times when it is appropriate to do exactly that.

Regardless of whether a higher price can send the message of exceptional value with your product or service, you should always avoid sounding apologetic or ashamed of your price merely because it is higher than someone else's.

Here are some samples of how some of my Elite Sellers would take pride in having the highest price:

> "I know that the figure I am going to quote you is much higher than what you had in mind. However, also keep in mind that this product is going to wipe out that difference by helping you make (save) much more money in the immediate future."

> "I just want you to know that there may be some sticker shock here. But, of course, the real shock is in the immense return that comes from one of the most important investments any firm can make."

"There are two surprises here. One, if you haven't shopped around lately, you may be a little surprised at the price. But... you'll also be pleasantly surprised when you see what this plan can do for you."

"We aren't the cheapest. But, nobody offers more for your money than we do."

"Not the lowest price, that's true...but, easily the best bargain (or value) you can find."

"Quality isn't cheap. We sell quality"

Price & Profit

Many buyers, especially in some industries or with some products, may have a tendency to try and negotiate for a lower price and will attempt to do so by asking that you either give up a portion of your fee, commission, or remuneration, or that you or your company forgo a portion of the profit from this buyer's sale. No excuse, be prepared!

First, it is beyond the scope of this text to examine legal issues relating to "full disclosure." You or your company should be well versed not only in what is legally required, but what is ethically appropriate. If, however, you have met both the legal and ethical requirements for disclosure, profit, or remuneration, then it's time to stand firm on your price. Doing so demands that you express pride in what you sell, the price that you charge, and your right to make a profit.

Here are some ideas on how to do this:

"Our price, like your business includes a reasonable profit margin. Our profit is your guarantee that we'll stay in business to take care of your service problem."

"I believe you agree that there is no sense in taking an order without making a profit. Would you trust a company that makes a habit of losing money?"

"You know better than I do that if a company lowers the price, the cut has to come from somewhere. Would you want us to shave off a little from your warranty? Would you want us to shave off a little from our service when you need it? I don't believe you would want us to do any of these things, right?"

"When you buy from us, we will make a small profit. But...we make it only once. You, on the other hand, will profit from this purchase for months to come."

"I know that there are some who would give you a kickback from their profits just to get your business. Take my word; all they did was quote an inflated price to do so. We don't do that. When your price is fair to begin with, it's the same for every customer."

"We don't lowball the price upfront and then spend our time trying to recoup it by reducing our service. Our company doesn't operate that way. I don't think yours does either, does it?"

"Our modest margin is far less than the added value we offer. If we don't recoup the loss on your sale from your service, we'll have to take it from another customer. We don't treat our customers that way and would ask that you not pressure us to do something you wouldn't do to your own customers."

Again, local or state laws may prevent rebating on some products or may set the sales commission or contingency fee for certain transactions. Of course, you should follow the law. If you sell for a company, you should also follow your employer's directions regarding how to handle buyer requests for you to reduce your personal commission or sales fee.

Price Concessions
With some products and under certain circumstances, there may be room for negotiation on price. But, Elite Sellers follow the rule of the successful negotiator by never, absolutely never, making the first offer. They let the request come from the buyer so they can

know what the buyer had in mind before telling the buyer what the seller had in mind. And, always, the Elite Seller, even if offering a small "price concession," will have a "catch" that the buyer first agrees to the deal.

"If I can get the home office to accept your request for free delivery, do we have a deal?"

"If our production department approves delivery without this feature, so we can reduce your investment commitment, will you okay this purchase today?"

"I'm sorry we can't change the price. But...we might be able to get you a better interest rate. What would you say if I tried to find a different premium finance company?"

"There is nothing I can do about the price. However, we might consider helping you with the payment terms. If I can get this approved, will you make this investment?"

"I'm sorry; the price is the price. The only thing we could consider is deferred billing. If I could get this for you, would you be ready to move on this today?"

"I can't change the price because I can't change the costs underlying that price, but how 'bout I make it easier for you to pay for it? If I can, are you interested?"

"Today's price is less than tomorrow's. If I can find a way to help you lock it in, would you be interested in moving before the end of the week?"

"I can move up the installation date; I can finance the purchase; I can provide you with top notch service, but...I can't lower the price. Seems like two out of three ain't bad. Do we have a deal?"

Chapter 15

OF FEAR, LEARNING & CRITICISM
If you find a path with no obstacles, it probably doesn't lead anywhere...Frank A. Clark

Now that you've learned all I can provide about face-to-face skills for Elite Status selling, it seems appropriate to address some of the less objective issues often critical to success. I believe, for example, that the single biggest barrier to success (at anything) may simply be fear in its many forms. In selling, it's more the direct and indirect results of fear—the fear of rejection that manifests itself in talking to strangers about something they may not wish to talk about, or in "convincing" strangers to do something you perceive they may not want to do. Some thoughts on overcoming the fear of rejection, learning from others, and how the 80/20 Rule can help you focus and succeed are appropriate.

The Pareto Principle
In 1906, Italian economist Vilfredo Pareto published a paper asserting that twenty percent of his country's people held eighty percent of his country's wealth. He went on to create a mathematical formula to help other governments analyze and predict similar inequalities. In the 30s and 40s, an American quality management pioneer, Dr. Joseph Juran, observed a standard he called the "vital few and trivial many" and, in doing so, it appeared he was applying Pa-

reto's observations to the corporate environment. For this reason, the name Pareto's Principle stuck to Juran's work (probably also because the alliteration made it sound better than Juran's Principle) and the "vital few and trivial many" faded from the public consciousness in favor of the Pareto Principle or what we commonly refer to today as the 80/20 Rule.

Eventually, more and more managers and corporations began to observe parallels in their own areas of expertise. When applied to selling, for example, the Pareto Principle says that 80 percent of a company's sales will come from 20 percent of its sellers. Or, 80 percent of sales revenues will come from 20 percent of the sales. Such observations help sales managers anticipate where the greatest room for improvement may be and thus where solutions would be more cost effective. As a seller, instead of focusing on the areas you enjoy or that others are focusing on, you can apply the 80/20 Rule to all that you do: from prospecting (80 percent of your sales will come from 20 percent of your prospects), to selling (80 percent of your time will be spent with 20 percent of your buyers), to revenues (80 percent of your commissions will come from 20 percent of your sales), to service (80 percent of your service problems will come from 20 percent of your existing clients). Using the 80/20 Rule as a guidepost can help anyone locate and analyze those problem areas where focused solutions often hold the greatest return...at least 80 percent of the time.

Fear of Rejection
The 80/20 Rule percentage is rarely exact (i.e. 85/15 or 90/10), but that doesn't diminish its application. My sales team often discussed how uncanny it was that month after month our sales reports seemed to confirm the Pareto Principle's relevance. Around 20 percent of the sellers in my company were making 80 percent of the sales and earning almost 80 percent of the commissions, while the remaining 80 percent were only selling around 20 percent; and even they seemed amazed at the mathematical consistency.

Keep in mind, depending on your method of calculation, this was a difference of almost 400 percent (80/20=4.00). In other words, among a group of sellers that all met the minimum requirements of my company, some (one in five) were selling four times more than (or four times better than) the entire rest of the company.

At first I thought such production disparity would create competition beneficial to the bottom line. As it turned out though, the 80 percent who were only selling 20 percent were more discouraged by their figures and their consistent position at the bottom of the company sales chart and thus, over time, they became frustrated or worse, complacent. Conversely, it appeared that the 20 percent who were selling 80 percent increased in confidence, became even more aggressive, taking more chances, and making even more sales as a group.

It was about this time I began to observe the impact that both self-esteem and fear of rejection could have on production. Fear in sales, as I mentioned, manifests itself mostly in talking to strangers or in being rejected by strangers either over the phone when asking for appointments, in face-to-face presentations when asking for the order, or in cold calling or contacting potential prospects. If not overcome, fear can be devastating to a career in selling. Even though my lower-end sellers were making lots of money and producing profit for the company, what little fear of rejection they had was being confirmed (and thus magnified) by their lower share of total company sales—and, for many, it only made them more reticent to ask for an order, to make cold calls, or to aggressively push a buyer to part with his or her money. In other words, they feared the failure that was seemingly inevitable. As a sales manager, I had to help them overcome whatever doubt or fear might be holding them back.

A potential solution came to me one night when my wife and I played the game Charades with dinner guests. In Charades, each person must act out the name of a movie, book, or TV show for members of their own team to guess. Great fun, but...two of the grown-ups were reluctant to stand in front of the small gathering and "possibly" embarrass themselves; initially, one flatly refused. Their children, on the other hand, were not only willing, but enthusiastic to do so. They easily threw caution entirely to the wind making complete fools of themselves in front of an intimidating audience of authority figures and strangers.

That's when it dawned on me—fear of rejection is learned, not inherited. We aren't born with it, we acquire it through experience. Like the grown-ups playing Charades, "some" of my low-end sellers had learned to fear rejection and their fear was confirmed by their usual position at the bottom of the company sales charts. With this realization it was easy to conclude that what had been learned could be unlearned or at least reduced by changing their daily experiences.

The Buddy System
During one quarter, I implemented a new program in which the most successful sellers would mentor those who were the least successful. During this three month period, selected sellers from the low-end group accompanied selected sellers from the higher producing group on sales calls to observe, to take notes, and…to unlearn their fears, though this was not the stated purpose. The group nicknamed it the "Buddy System."

At the quarterly sales meeting immediately following its implementation, the room was abuzz with conversation. Everyone was sharing stories about their joint sales calls, problem buyers, product drawbacks, and a host of new experiences. Most of those in the lower producing group were excited about selling again and about getting back into their own territories and competing to be part of the higher group. But, here's the important part: the reason for their excitement was not that they learned new skills or new prospecting techniques, which many did, but that they saw how the higher level producers were rejected, lost sales, or simply failed to get the order, but…were not discouraged by it. They were not afraid to continue talking to strangers, asking for appointments, cold calling, and closing sales. In fact, just knowing that more successful sellers faced rejection without fearing it made the lower end sellers more aware of their inherent fear and how unfounded it was.

I may never know the reason, perhaps it was just the attention everyone was getting, but…the next quarterly report showed the highest increase in production over a previous quarter in the company's short history. Of course, there will always be those who don't close as many sales as others, roughly. But, I found that the 80/20 Rule not only told me where to concentrate my efforts as a sales manager, it also led me to learn that self-esteem and fear of rejection were things a sales manager could actually change. If closing sales, asking for the order, or otherwise pushing someone to do something you perceive they do not wish to do is a problem for you, I suggest you spend some time observing and partnering with someone who is successful. It's likely you'll find the biggest difference isn't how many times you are rejected, but how your fear of being rejected alters your behavior.

Constructive Criticism

The Buddy System experiment had its challenges. Some were less open to peer learning than others. Often the problem in acquiring the experience of others more talented than ourselves lies in our ego or the ability to be truly open to criticism, constructive or otherwise. When it comes to changing the way we are, or the way we behave, it's often second nature to simply not see what others are doing or hear what they are saying.

To maximize the benefit of peer feedback, Carnegie Mellon Professor Randy Pausch developed a spreadsheet based on each student's confidential impression of other students when working together in group projects. At semester's end, after each student had completed five different collaborative projects with three different teammates on each, he was able to rank every student based on whether his/her peers found them easy or difficult to work with. Was he/she a team player? Did he/she listen and learn from others?

One talented student that the others found particularly obnoxious was unfazed by his ranking in the lowest quartile because, in typical fashion, he was convinced he was at the top of that quartile. In his own self-absorbed mind, therefore, that meant he was almost in the next higher quartile, not really in the bottom one. And that meant he was close to 50 percent or right in the middle of the entire class, which really meant his peers thought he was doing "just fine."

"I'm so glad we had this talk," Pausch told him, "because I think it's important that I give you some specific information. You are not just in the bottom 25 percent. Out of 50 students in the class, your peers ranked you dead last. You are number 50. You have a serious issue. They say you're not listening. You're hard to get along with. Things are not going well."

That may have been the most valuable lesson an otherwise very talented computer science student at Carnegie Mellon could've learned. The point is that the "most" talented people are always those who start with talent and then benefit from the feedback of other talented people.

Don't wait for a detailed spreadsheet and a frank conversation with a concerned college professor. Don't wait for your sales manager to implement a Buddy System. Neither are likely to ever come. Instead, embrace criticism. Sift through polite comments to find the real truth. Implement your own Buddy System by being open to constructive observations rendered by qualified peers.

Before moving on to Platform II, you may want to review all of the skills taught in Platform I by consulting the Appendix.

PLATFORM II

Group Presentations

and Proposals

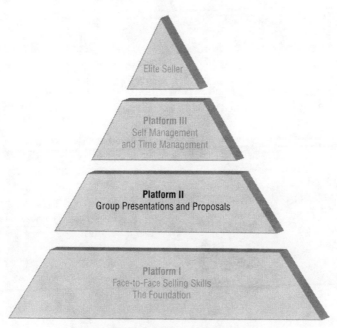

PLATFORMS OF SUCCESS

Chapter 16

PRESENTATIONS & PROPOSALS

A speech without a purpose is like a journey without a destination...unknown

Now that we've learned the basics of Elite Selling—which for our purposes was usually performed on someone sitting behind a desk—it's time to transfer those same basics to selling to a group, which is, more than likely, sitting around a boardroom table or seated in a classroom or convention hall.

If you are an Elite Seller, inevitably you'll be asked at some point to present your product to the managers or decision makers of a business or company. This will happen if for no other reason than any good CEO or decision maker often seeks input from other trusted employees when making important business-wide decisions.

While the face-to-face skills of Elite Sellers—those of uncovering needs, selling benefits, handling attitudes, and closing the sale—are also woven through any group sales presentation, the circumstances, logistics, and dynamics of group selling warrant a different approach; one that relies less on questioning and listening, and more on your ability to speak (and sell), while others are questioning and listening.

The Greeks
The ancient Greeks were among the first to study the art of persuasion through presentations and public debate. The cornerstones of a good sales presentation today are no different than the three they codified thousands of years ago; they are: Ethos, Pathos, and Logos.

1.)   Ethos—Character and Credibility

2.)   Pathos—Emotion and Delivery

3.)   Logos—Logic and Content

Ethos is the trust element in most sales presentations. How credible is the presenter and how credible are the facts which he or she is presenting? The customer attitude of Skepticism is more prevalent or more likely to be encountered during presentations where the element of Ethos has been ignored or compromised by either the presenter's style or the design and substance of the presentation.

Pathos may be the most important element of a successful persuasive presentation. It is the presenter's enthusiasm and emotion and thus demonstrated belief in what he or she is saying. Almost without exception, those whom I instructed who had passion for their product or business and who were able to let it come through during stand up talks were the successful presenters. They injected personal stories and found relevant examples that involved their audience and made them laugh or identify with the seller/presenter. The less successful presenters were often unbalanced, focusing too much on the features or facts of the product. While their audiences may have been informed, they were often left unmoved.

Logos is the rational communication that takes place between a room full of buyers and a sales presenter. It deals not only with the logical flow of the presentation and the arrangement of main points, but it also involves the credibility of the information itself and the sources of proof and substantiation for important features or benefits.

A good sales presentation balances the Greek cornerstones of Ethos, Pathos, and Logos into a well blended conveyance of thought and energy that is logical, emotional, and easy to understand and which motivates the audience in a desired direction.

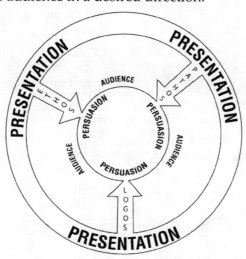

All Greek To Me

I'd like to ask your indulgence while I relate some background, which is based on personal, but hopefully relevant experience.

It was November of 1974 when I accepted my second job after college. It was with a state trade association whose members were independent property and casualty insurance agents—The Florida Association of Insurance Agents. I was 24 years old and had been hired to develop and teach a course in how to sell—basically to teach insurance agents how to do what they were already doing and which I had never done myself.

The prospect of standing before professional "sellers" (albeit novices in most cases) and telling them how to do their jobs better would intimidate the most seasoned sales trainer. I (a rookie), on the other hand, was petrified. My anxiety was rooted in three personal shortcomings: a lack of experience presenting to groups, a lack of knowledge in the subject matter at hand (selling), and a lack of knowledge about the subject to be sold (insurance).

In other words, I needed training in how to train, in how to present, and in how to handle the myriad of insurance technical questions I'd be asked by licensed insurance agents and be unable to answer.

One of the first things I did was sign up to take a course in public speaking from the Dale Carnegie Institute. Carnegie's training had a reputation for helping young or inexperienced presenters find confidence in front of audiences—the element of Pathos. One of the primary points driven home early in the program was that those who make presentations, whether it is to sell a product, to inform, or merely to entertain, must have earned the right to speak on the subject matter. Nothing, anywhere, can give someone more confidence in public speaking than knowing that they know more about the subject matter than anyone who will be listening to them speak. And nothing fulfills the goal of Pathos like confidence. This is especially true, I've found, when the presentation is to be interactive with questions or statements from the audience interspersed with your talk.

Thus, after Carnegie, I spent the better part of six months reading every book on "selling" I could find. Initially, we purchased structured training programs from the pioneer of the role-play approach, Xerox Learning Systems. Called *Personal Selling Skills*, the Xerox programs were designed around cassette tapes that featured realistic selling situations. Much of what I was to later develop had its genesis in the training of Xerox Learning Systems. I also watched videos and attended training seminars all over the country; every one I could. Until, eventually, I developed my own techniques and a presentation, which I rehearsed religiously. Ultimately, I began teaching three-day seminars and videotaping student role-plays. I spent ten years teaching at least one such course each month until, eventually, I was offered another challenge, equally daunting, and for which I was also woefully unprepared.

Small Groups
In 1983, I was drafted into service for a small software company and given the title vice president of Sales & Marketing. I was to recruit, hire, train, and motivate a sales force across 12 states initially.

The training involved teaching new recruits about the product and helping them acquire proficiency using the selling skills covered in Platform I.

Initially, however, my primary directive was to beat the competition by gaining the endorsement of our automated insurance policy rating system through presentations I would have to make to boards of directors of state associations representing independent insurance agents—the counterparts of the Florida association where I had been teaching sales training for the previous ten years.

Managing Logistics

Another charge I was given was to make similar presentations to the top executives of America's largest insurance carriers. I was to convince them to purchase the system and give it (or subsidize its purchase) to insurance agents contracted to sell for the company. One insurer bought 1,000 systems after such a presentation and put the money in an escrow account from which my company could withdraw as the systems were installed in agents' offices—agents I could convince to accept the company's offer.

I had nothing to do with the design or development of the product, so I'm not bragging when I tell you it was, for its time, light-years ahead of the competition. It was a captivating automated, dial-up, download comparative rating system that held audiences, small and large, completely spellbound. It developed final premiums for all lines of property and casualty insurance, virtually instantaneously, after data entry. And, it compared the rates for any number of insurance companies, actually printing out proposals with the final figures for presentation to clients or those buyers of auto, home, business, and other lines of coverage.

Slick, yes...but in the early 1980s such an electronic marvel didn't come cheap and worse, it was greeted with complete skepticism by a market replete with those who had never owned a computer and had absolutely no desire to do so. Achieving ultimate Logos was a major challenge in such an environment. Skepticism, Indifference, and Objection were customer attitudes I became quite proficient at handling. But...that's another story.

129

To gain the endorsements of state agent associations, I had to make the contact; get the executive director to call a board meeting (or attend an already scheduled one); make a presentation of the automated system; describe the benefits that would accrue to the association in terms of royalties, membership retention, and member relations (if they endorsed it); and close the sale with either a formal vote of endorsement on the spot or the promise of such a vote in the reasonable near future. Following the good time management principles discussed in Unit III, I focused initially on the bigger states, where an endorsement would yield a bigger payout because more insurance agents would be potential purchasers of the program.

Later, after (if) an endorsement was gained, I would return to each state and travel from one city to the next, presenting the product to small local groups of independent property and casualty insurance agents—members of the endorsing association. My goal at these presentations was to sign up as many subscribers to the software as I could. Thanks to closing the sale with the one carrier mentioned above, I was able to tell about 1,000 agents it was free, though they needed to purchase hardware, including external modems, hard drives, printers, etc.

As we'll see in this unit, I learned what to do, and what not to do while using graphics to augment a presentation. Compared to today's laptops and PowerPoint-style presentations with projection systems the size of alarm clocks, the logistics I faced in 1983 were mind boggling. I had to use what was called an RGB (red, green, and blue) Projection Unit. These were the oldest of projectors using light emanating from three bulbs, each a different color. The colors blended on a projection screen and reproduced the images from a small CRT screen attached to an old style table top computer operated by either me or my assistant. Needless to say, the Red, Green, and Blue never seemed to line up on the main screen, leaving a vibrating image and a squinting audience. Still, we presented the functions of the system—the price, the service contract, the required hardware, the monthly download fee. Then…we asked for a deposit check to…"Lock in today's price!" The presentation usually took close to two hours, which included time for questions. Then, it was on to the next city, day after every weekday, and then, on Fridays, to the nearest airport for the plane back home to see my wife and son.

On the plane, I usually performed the last task for each trip, which was to write down what went wrong and what went right, and how best to share it with others.

Of course, the pace was grueling and had its price, both emotional and physical. For well over a year, I left my home in Tallahassee, virtually every Sunday evening, flying far and wide, and returned the following Friday night, usually late. I either gave presentations to boards, asking for their endorsement, or I gave statewide demos to small groups of insurance agent members of associations whose boards had already voted to endorse the product, detouring occasionally to Hartford, Chicago, New York, or Baltimore in order to present to the executive board of a large insurance carrier.

I was miserable, never at home, under a lot of stress, and my family life suffered. I recall my frequent flyer miles were so high my co-workers joked I could probably redeem them for a ticket on the next space shuttle.

At the end of eighteen months, I had presented a comparative insurance policy rating system to the board of directors for 35 state independent agents associations, gaining the endorsement of 25, or half of the total. Importantly, they were the big states—California, Texas, New York, New Jersey, Pennsylvania, Ohio, Georgia, Massachusetts. In most weeks, I presented twice a day: once in the morning, then once in the afternoon after driving to another city. Thousands of small independent businesses wrote checks during the statewide tours that followed their state association's endorsement; this, even though the product would usually not be available for purchase in their state for many months.

I take pride in the time management that was required to schedule and present the product to so many groups, boards, and individuals under such challenging circumstances. I was equally proud to learn that I had the skill necessary to persuade some to part with their money. The skills were not mine, however; they were those I garnered from the Elite Students who had attended one or more of the sales seminars I had been teaching for the previous ten years or that I had saved in my diary of Elite Skills after listening to hundreds of videotaped role-plays. I was thrilled to have an opportunity to actually put to practice what I had been teaching and learning for almost a decade. It was during this time that I figured I made over 200 sales presentations and began to quantify what was right, wrong, and in between with every step in the process. The more I did it, the better I got at doing it. And the better I got at doing it, the more sales I made, and the more information I could share with my sales team or catalogue to share with others…someday.

The Presentation
Initially, my hard copy presentation was strong on Ethos and Logos, but weak on Pathos. It was designed to meet the basic requirements of the group as to price, functionality, benefits vs. features. But it did not entertain. It didn't move my listeners. As I made more presentations, I became more comfortable and began to take more chances. The more chances I took, the more sales I closed — and the more I learned about what worked and what didn't work when selling to a small crowd.

I began to make modifications after every presentation in order to correct deficiencies — deficiencies I was sure weren't present the first time I assembled my presentation and materials. I asked co-workers to listen and critique what was being said and how I said it, and uncovered other deficiencies, large and small. Eventually, I arrived at a proposal form and format that had everything I needed to be able to say the right things, in the right way, the first time.

The layout and design of the "hard copy" document was tailored to the audience, and met the admonitions I now take for granted. It was short, although there was a substantial appendix filled with references and proof sources, sample contracts, and the like. And, it was in the right format.

But, your lesson starts here with a list of the ten problems I encountered and that are found in most sales presentations I hear today.

1.)   They are too long.

2.)   They are too complicated.

3.)   They sell only features.

4.)   They are poorly structured.

5.)   Materials have errors, both typographical and technical.

6.)   Materials are amateurish or poorly designed.

7.)   They don't offer proof for the important points.

8.)   Audience management is lacking.

9.)   The presenter has an uninspiring delivery.

10.) There is no commitment requested of the audience.

While the above items are not listed in order of importance, I do believe that the two most important overriding considerations for any presentation are the first two—length and simplicity. They magnify the faults. Any and all of the other deficiencies appear larger and are more impacting if the first two are not governing during the design and delivery of any presentation. Therefore, before we talk about how to prepare and deliver a presentation to avoid the ten deficiencies above, it's appropriate to comment on both brevity and simplicity.

Brevity
Frank Bettger made more than 40,000 sales calls in his career. So successful was he at turning around his career in selling that he wrote a book, *How I Raised Myself From Failure to Success in Selling*, which Dale Carnegie said was "the most helpful and inspiring book on salesmanship that I have ever read." As to the importance of brevity in persuading groups to your point of view, Bettger offered the following true story.

Back in the days when Mark Twain was piloting boats up and down the Mississippi, the Rock Island Railroad decided to build a bridge across that great span between Rock Island, Illinois, and Davenport, Iowa. The steamboat companies were quite prosperous and intent on keeping it that way. Wheat, dry goods, leather, tools, guns and other products which our early settlers were able to produce were trekked to the Mississippi by ox teams and covered wagons, and then shipped down the river. The owners of steamboats saw their right to use the river as inalienable and guarded it jealously.

If the railroad were to build a bridge all manner of unfair competition might occur. The railroads might prosper to the steamship owner's detriment. The bridge itself might even hinder the passing of ships. Fearing all manner of harm if the railroad succeeded in building the bridge, the steamship owners entered an injunction in the courts to prevent its construction and then filed a huge lawsuit to end the problem once and for all. The wealthy steamboat owners hired the best lawyer they could find, the very famous and talented Judge Wead whose presence, along with the facts, were to turn the case into one of the most important precedents in transportation history. On the closing day of the trial Judge Wead waxed eloquent as he held the crowed spellbound for two hours. He even hinted of dissolution of the Union by reason of this fierce controversy. At the close of his oration, loud applause could be heard across the courthouse grounds.

When the lawyer for the Rock Island Railroad rose to speak, the audience felt sorry for him. He was scraggly, not well dressed. And, he didn't deliver a lengthy oratory. He spoke only 60 seconds. Here is substantially what he said:

"First, I want to congratulate my opponent upon his wonderful oration. I have never heard a finer speech. But, gentlemen of the jury, Judge Wead has obscured the main issue. After all, the demands of those who travel from east to west are no less important than those who navigate up and down the river. The only question for you to decide is whether a man has more right to travel up and down the river than he has to cross the river."

Then he sat down.

It didn't take the jury long to reach a decision, a decision in favor of this poorly dressed, long, lanky obscure country lawyer. His name was Abraham Lincoln.

Lincoln was one of the greatest presenters of all time and was a master of brevity. He often used it as tool to convince others that what he was saying must be right because it didn't take so long to say it. When Lincoln made the most famous address in the history of the world, it was, again, after the man who preceded him had spoken for two hours. Lincoln spoke exactly two minutes. Nobody remembers what Edward Everett said, or even who he was, but Abraham Lincoln's Gettysburg Address will live forever. Everett's opinion of the speech Lincoln gave was written in a note he sent to Lincoln the next day. "I should be glad if I could flatter myself that I came as near to the central idea of the occasion in two hours, as you did in two minutes."

Can you sense from this story how influencing merely being brief can be? As we develop rules for developing successful sales presentations to boards or groups of decision makers, it's important to compare everything that is said to Lincoln's penchant for brevity. If you are able to convey the central theme of your presentation in fewer words, in less time, than those who are selling against you, then I would say you have approached the next plateau in the sales cycle with one leg up over your competitors. Of course, the secret to being brief is closely tied to the skill of simplification.

Simplicity
Ben Feldman (1912–1993) was an American businessman and one of the most prolific sellers in world history. I referenced his techniques in Unit I and you may want to Google his story for a bit of inspiration.

Born in New York City, Feldman was one of nine children of recent immigrant parents. He was short, fat, bald, and spoke with a pronounced lisp, but...in 1975 he sold more than $116 million of "individual" life insurance policies. While, thanks to decades of inflation, that might not seem like much today, at the time it was so unbelievable as to be doubted by anyone who heard it. It was, in fact, more individual life insurance than was sold by two-thirds of the life insurance companies in America.

Feldman's approach was unique. He religiously followed the KISS Principle, or...Keep It Sweet and Simple! He exploited his own knack for taking the most complicated financial concepts and reducing them to everyday examples. He did it in such a way that even grade-schoolers could understand. He believed in using analogies to sell his intangible product and he looked for opportunities to add color, metaphor, and personal anecdotes to spice his boardroom presentations. The analogy of the "feather" used in Platform I to describe how procrastinating the buying of life insurance is like accumulating feathers in your pocket is the perfect example of Feldman's style. He never dwelled on the complicated or the technical side of what he was selling and was a master at transforming stale material into a motivational dialogue between seller and buyer.

Never wax technical merely to dazzle. It may feel good to you, but...not to the buyers. Others with Feldman's physical limitations would have overcompensated, perhaps, hoping to distract buyers and groups of buyers with technical acumen. Feldman did the opposite and sold $1.8 billion of insurance for New York Life from 1942 to his death in 1993 and still holds the world record for the most product sold (by value adjusted for inflation) by any salesman in a career; in one year he sold $100 million and, in a single day, $20 million in individual life insurance policies. Near the end of his career, his annual renewal commissions exceeded $1,000,000. His axiom, Keep It Sweet and Simple, has been followed by the most successful sellers in history ever since, and it is, in my opinion, paramount in giving effective boardroom sales presentations.

Winging It

But, it is the need for brevity and simplicity that make sales presentations so challenging to some. Add these challenges to the fear of public speaking and you've got a task that, even for the most disciplined and confident executive, can be downright overwhelming. For seasoned veterans, who through repetition and longevity have overcome the fear, there's still anxiety on how to create the most potent presentation when it really matters—before an important group. Where do you begin? How do you decide what to include? How do you make sure it's not too long or too short, or that its Pathos, Logos, or Ethos are appropriate?

Frankly, designing a sales presentation, keeping it brief, following the KISS Principle and avoiding the remaining eight deficiencies listed above is sometimes so daunting it's easy to put off; until, eventually, there's no time left and you wind up "winging it." For the very rare individual, this may be okay—not the best, but...just okay. While we may admire someone who is "good on their feet," it is better to admire someone who is good and prepared while on their feet. Even the best of presenters is better when prepared and rehearsed. I have encountered no exceptions to this rule.

For those with a tendency to put off daunting tasks and who desire to avoid the ten deficiencies above, I've put together some steps for you to follow. Regardless of any other distractions or deterrents, if you merely follow these steps, in the order and manner prescribed, I promise you'll arrive at a well-designed and inspirational presentation. Once you have the framework in place, we'll delve into some additional hints and suggestions that can give your presentation style an edge over the competition.

Chapter 17

FOLLOW THE STEPS

...The best impromptu speeches are the ones written well in advance...Ruth Gordon, actress

Again, the following steps, if followed one at a time, will not only help you avoid the pitfalls of most presenters, but...will help you overcome any tendency to procrastinate or put off the task.

For those convinced they are among the "elite" who can "wing" presentations with little or no preparation, I ask that you indulge me and this process. Give the following steps a chance. Isolate one or two that may be of benefit. Adapt others that may help improve what you are already good at doing. What have you got to lose?

Step #1—State the purpose of the presentation and make a list of the important points and sub-points you want to make.
There are many reasons why so many presentations are too long. In my case, I often tried to tell the audience everything I wanted them to hear, rather than only what they "needed" or "wanted" to hear. I wasted time, their time, talking about "features" that I couldn't convert into benefits, at least not for that audience. Nor was I allowing enough time for questions, or enough time for visuals, or improvisational anecdotes, or enough time for pauses in my presentation. In fact, I often found myself out of time entirely, while the

competition waited outside for their turn and my listeners became more concerned about my encroachment on my competitor's time than about my presentation or my product.

The Purpose—All presentations, regardless of their complexity, are designed with a single purpose. Whether that purpose is to sell, educate, or to entertain, state that purpose to yourself at the beginning of the development process. Write it out if necessary and put it at the top of your draft outline or at the top of your list of important points you'll use to develop that outline. Keep this purpose in mind always as it is the benchmark for accepting or rejecting the points, sub-points, proof sources, transition language, and closing comments of your presentation. Initially, the presentations I gave were poorly planned and lacked the benefits of rehearsal; and worse, without the purpose at the fore, they meandered off point into areas that distracted from the buying process.

Of course, your purpose in a sales presentation is, in the end, to make the sale. But, your presentation may only be a step towards the achievement of that end goal. It might be that your presentation's purpose is only to stimulate enough interest to warrant a feasibility study or an invitation to put together a more detailed proposal. It might be that your presentation is to convince the buyers to purchase a particular model or version of your product, or to keep your product or service instead of changing to a competitor who has, unfortunately slipped his/her foot in "your" door. Point: keep your purpose in mind as you design your presentation. Don't fall into the trap of merely making the same presentation you always make or merely adapting a face-to-face sales call to a group environment.

Key Points—With the purpose clearly in mind, you should start by making an exhaustive list of the points that could be made. Based on your experience as an Elite Seller, determine what advantages you have over the competition—what benefits your product or service has, which are either important to buyers or are likely to be influential in their buying decision. Sometimes informal questions by phone or an initial interview can give you information that may be important to the buyer's unique situation.

Some sellers use a questionnaire to formalize this process or to find all of the key problems or concerns of the buyer's company or business. Sometimes a formal survey or questionnaire provides you with information about the company's needs that even the company and its employees didn't realize they had. Or, better yet, you can uncover solutions to problems they were unable to solve. Sharing such diagnostics during a sales presentation truly ingratiates any seller to his/her audience, especially if they've got to buy your product to implement those solutions.

Limit the Points
Despite having an exhaustive list, you should aim to communicate a maximum of four key messages successfully rather than many poorly. Your preparation and delivery will benefit from having fewer key messages, and your audience will more easily grasp your critical themes and ideas. If you have to communicate more than four messages, perhaps consider doing two separate presentations, combining two or more points into one, or find another way of getting these other messages across (perhaps via a leave-behind piece, handout, or e-mail).

Your list of important points (benefits) should be developed from a more exhaustive list of all possible benefits. Even if you aren't doing a group presentation, it's sometimes a good exercise to put everything down on paper. Then, consolidate the master list into the broadest possible categories and keep those categories down to only three or four points, but, in any event, never more than five.

For example, if you are presenting an automation system to a corporate board of directors, you could divide it into five sections: Functionality, Price, Service, Commitment, and Dependability. If you are presenting a real estate deal to a board of county commissioners, it could be: Price, Location, Appreciation, and Building Codes. For an insurance presentation to the oversight committee of a condominium association, Premium, Coverage, Claims, and Agent Service could be the highlights. The point is to be as broad as possible and then to use the related sub-points to buttress, prove, or illustrate the main benefit.

Step #2—Develop an outline arranging your main points in a logical and appropriate sequence, placing sub-points, also in a logical and appropriate sequence, beneath them.

Often, the novice merely converts the usual face-to-face sales call to a group environment, allowing only for the differing logistics of a group format. This rarely works. In a group environment, points need to be presented in some order. Much like a story, they need to build on previous points. Often they can only be understood, fully, once other information has first been shared. Face-to-face sales calls that focus on listening to the customer rarely flow in a story board fashion. Presentations to groups, on the other hand, must always do so.

Winston Churchill once said he developed outlines of his presentations, but rarely consulted them. "I carry fire insurance, but I don't expect my house to burn down," he said. An outline is the same way; it's a reference that guides you through your presentation. It isn't supposed to be read.

Outlines have two basic benefits: one, they help presenters/sellers organize their important content and points; and two, they can help you remember what to say and often how to say it. An outline is more like a blue print for a bridge; you can actually build a model, look at it, modify it, and test its strength before you and your audience cross it together. Presentations with outlines are well planned, not "canned." They are guides, not "crutches." An outline keeps you from straying from the point and from having a presentation that is longer, wordier, or that violates one or more of the other ten deficiencies itemized above. They help clarify the structure during the design stage and can be used as your presentation notes and a handout for your listeners when appropriate.

Story Telling—I learned and began to categorize the differences in group or boardroom presentations vs. face-to-face one-on-one selling that I knew so well. The Elite Sales approach we discussed earlier, referred to as "getting around the bases," is present, but modified for someone who, by virtue of the environment, must do much of the talking. While listening is important, and while questions are an effective tool in boardroom presentations, the focus is more on what you say first in order to stimulate interest and questions from your audience. As we saw in step one, the information gathering stage has been completed and you are "presenting" decision makers a "proposal" developed from the information you already have or have assumed is relevant to this audience.

Of course, if all you had to do was just list the benefits for your audience, you could hand out the list and leave the room. But, you need to do some selling, and to sell to a group you often need to be a good storyteller. You need to create pictures in the buyer's mind or excite their imagination.

Before we talk about structuring your outline, let's consider how to put imagination into your sales story and increase your closing opportunities. Ask yourself the following questions about each of the benefits you'll be talking about. Then, encompass the appropriate message within each point in your final outline.

1.) What's the *most probing question* I could ask about this feature and benefit to stimulate the audience and gain their participation?

2.) What's the *most colorful statement* I could make about this feature and benefit?

3.) What's the *most demonstrative visual aide* I could use to illustrate this feature and benefit?

4.) What's the most *provocative proof source*, story, or example I can offer to back up the statements I make on this point or subpoint?

5.) Do I have all the most *impressive testimonials* with me? Are they the ones most likely to be accepted by the group?

6.) What is the *most impressive tabletop demonstration* that can be devised to impress the group on this point or sub-point?

7.) What is the *most compelling logic* I can find in relating this feature and benefit to others?

8.)   What *customer participation* can I devise in this feature and benefit so the group joins with me in the presentation?

9.)   What *on-site test* can I suggest for proving the validity of this point made during the presentation?

Outline Structure—The major points of a presentation outline are organized alphabetically or by Roman numeral: A, B, C, D, etc., or I, II, III, IV, etc. After you develop your main points, put subheadings under each one. Keep them simple and easy to read at a glance. Subheadings or supporting points are usually the opposite of what is chosen for the major points; numbers follow letters, letters follow numbers, and alternate down from there, indenting as you go. For example, beneath the letter A, B, or C, etc., you could indent the numbers 1, 2, 3, etc. Then, beneath each sub-point, you can revert to lower case letters again, a, b, c, etc.

I like to start with Roman numerals and then move to the alphabet and then back and forth between numbers and letters from there. But, it doesn't really matter. Some great presenters use bullet points only and merely indent each subset of points. Others use bullets, then asterisks, then the pound sign. What matters is the logical arrangement of the material and, once it is in hard copy, your ability to review, rearrange, and remove the unnecessary from your outline. With each point, have two or three pieces of support such as examples, definitions, testimony, or statistics. Keep in mind, indeed review, each of the questions described in the previous section for each of the points in your outline.

Using Your Outline—For smaller groups or less formal presentations, I often use my outline as a handout. Of course, if you are going to hand out the outline as an audience document, it should be numbered and alphabetized for the sake of clarity instead of just bullet points. It's also important to number the pages of your outline. Usually, I have an appendix attached that contains proof sources, graphs or charts, and other backup information to which I can refer the group as we follow the main outline together.

I'm sure to leave adequate space between each outline point so that listeners can write in notes. I even tell them that's what the space is for. I sometimes get them involved by telling them to underline something in my outline because it's important or because "we'll come back to it in a minute" or for whatever reason I can think of. Sometimes I just say, "now, write this down" or "write down this word in the margin, because it's key to this point." In this way, my "speakers notes" become an interactive audience slide show with one big difference from most visuals or PowerPoint presentations... there is no possibility of electronic failure or visibility problems.

Regardless of how you decide to use it, or even if you develop visual aides or a complimentary PowerPoint presentation, your original outline might look something like the following:

I. Introduction and Overview
    A. Your name and position
    B. Corporate name, background, and history
        1. Year founded
        2. Financial track record
        3. Current industry standing
            a. Standard & Poor's rankings
            b. SEC filings
    C. Purpose of presentation
        1. To reveal important benefits of going with the XYZ company
        2. To demonstrate the long-term savings possible
        3. To prove that service and responsiveness will not be a problem from XYZ.

II. Key Product Benefits
    A. Savings
    B. Functionality
    C. Service
    D. Future upgradeability

III. Savings
    A. Upfront cost

1. Deposit & Rebate
   a. Only 10% of sales price
   b. Balance only upon complete satisfaction
   c. Rebate available after 12 months
      i. Online form completion
      ii. Toll-free service number

   Etc.
   ↓

Graphics—Many presenters today use PowerPoint to dress up their presentations. Most board rooms and other presentation facilities are equipped to handle such and we'll talk more about how to use this and other graphic tools later. However, the beauty of PowerPoint and other presentation software is that they can double as your presentation outline and sometimes can be identical to it.

In this way, you can avoid holding or referencing a piece of paper. However, it has its drawbacks—visibility, for example, or the fact that you can only skip from one screen to another. With a physical outline, you can look at your entire speech at once and everyone can see every word no matter where they are sitting. You can direct everyone to any numbered page instantaneously. For this reason, when using PowerPoint or other electronic media, always keep a physical outline handy as backup and as a tool for your audience in case the computer, the battery, the power, the lighting, whatever, doesn't perform as intended.

Step #3—Write out your introductory comments and your opening Initial Benefit Statement.
Before we talk about an Initial Benefit Statement, let's look at your opening comments as these are probably among the most important words you will speak—important enough to write down, rehearse, rewrite and re-rehearse again, until you are absolutely comfortable with what you will say when the audience turns its undivided attention to…"you."

The opening of the presentation sets the stage for what is to follow. Participants are introduced and the purpose of the presentation is stated. Good opening comments usually include your name, title, relevant experience. If you are introduced by someone else and this information is already shared with the audience, then thank your introducer and tell them how long you are planning on speaking. Tell them what you are going to be speaking about. You should also present a VERY BRIEF summary or outline of the points to be covered. This helps keep your audience become oriented properly within the framework of your script.

Start Strong—It's surprising to me how many presenters fumble around at the beginning. They start with something like "Okay, well...maybe we should go ahead and get started." Or, "If everyone is here, would it be okay if we begin?"

I prefer taking charge with something like "Hi, my name is [Scott Johnson] and it's good to be here. We are going to be talking about..." You can even rehearse making sure those are the absolute first words you say out loud.

You can follow the introduction with something to get the attention of the audience if you like. This might be a startling statement, statistic, or your own story; humor, very brief humor, can work well at this point, but isn't a requirement. Listeners pay close attention when a person begins with, "You know, there's an intersection right down the street and one morning the traffic light wasn't working..." You could mention something you read in the papers that morning if it's relevant. Asking a question is another way to make people listen. "How many of you would like to save more money each year?" Or, "how many of you think you deserve a raise?"

I used to use the "by show of hands, how many believe..." technique. And I'd even raise my hand to show them what I wanted them to do and to stimulate wider hand raising or participation. Then, I'd follow immediately with another question, again raising my own hand; and then, again, the same pattern, until, after several questions, I finished with "okay, how many aren't going to raise their hand no matter what stupid question I ask?" to which several who hadn't previously responded would usually raise their hands.

It was humorous, participatory, and it got the audience awake and involved. Whatever technique you use, if you grab the attention of the audience you are on your way to a successful speech.

Initial Benefit Statements—You'll notice that this particular step says to write out your introductory comments and your Initial Benefit Statement.

Recall from previous lessons that a General Benefit Statement is nothing more than the process of introducing benefits without using questions in order to direct, or redirect, the sales call. You may also remember we talked about question statements and Initial Benefit Statements, which are used for the same purpose, the latter for the beginning of the sales call. In group presentations, they are the same except there's no need to wait for a response that will ultimately lead to a Specific Benefit Statement. You merely proceed with the outline of your presentation. Again, there are two steps to a General or Initial Benefit Statement; they are:

1.) State an assumed need or problem of the buyer or buyer's company.

2.) Describe a general benefit of your product which addresses that need based on problems and background information you have gathered prior to the presentation. Use proof if necessary, appropriate, and convenient.

Knowing that the existing system's provider had gone out of business and was therefore unable to fulfill its service commitment and training requirements as well as future system upgrades, a software seller decided to stress the financial status and solvency of his company by saying:

1.) "It's extremely important in today's world to know that your vendor will be around to fulfill the promises that made you decide to buy your system from them in the first place.

2.) "XYZ Systems, Inc. has been in business for over 30 years and is the oldest network company in the Southeast. We are listed on the New York Stock Exchange and our last quarterly earnings statement showed a return on equity in the top five percent of our industry group. In other words, you'll have the peace of mind knowing that what I promise, XYZ will be around to deliver."

For good measure, you could add:

"In the back of your materials, you'll find a copy of our last quarterly statement and a Standard & Poor's analysis of XYZ's profit picture."

At this point, you're off and running and can use an appropriate segue to move to another General Benefit Statement for your next point(s).

Step #4—Write out the General Benefit Statements you will use to introduce each point of your presentation and develop transitional language to move you from one point to the next.
This is the part of the script in which the bulk of the subject matter is presented. The body of a long presentation should be separated into smaller, easily assimilated modules or benefit statements based on each single point, idea or benefit. These sub-sections should each have their own simple opening, body, and summary.

Once you have a General Benefit Statement for each of your points, you can tie your points together with transition statements. These could be basic landmarks such as "First," "Second," "Next," or "Finally." I almost always use what's called an internal summary; that is, I simply include the point I just made and tell what I plan to talk about next. For example, you could say:

Now that we have seen how the finances and the installation would work, let's move on to the training module. There are three concepts in XYZ's training that make us different from all others, they are…etc.

When you have an introduction, two or three main points with support for each, appropriate transitions, and a conclusion, you basically have your entire speech organized in a way that the audience can easily follow.

Proof—And remember, this is a sales presentation. You are trying to be persuasive. Ethos, or credibility, is imperative, particularly on important points. There's no need to overdo it or belabor every detail, but…if it's important enough to mention, then it's important enough to have some proof or verification on hand—particularly if the proof is easy enough to develop or secure.

Expert testimonials are particularly effective and reflect RASSCL Principle #2—Authority. For example, if I were discussing the financial soundness of an insurance company, I might mention that close to five percent of all insurers go bankrupt annually and another 20 percent are considered "at risk" according to financial rating agencies. Or, I might simply give an example of what happened to a friend of mine when his insurance carrier was placed in receivership. By using stories, testimony, and statistics, you add depth to your evidence, thus enhancing the persuasiveness and Ethos of your presentation.

Social Proof—RASSCL Principle #4. The concept of Social Proof, is even more relevant in group presentations, in my opinion, than in face to face calls. In their studies, Cialdini, Goldstein, and Martin showed how powerful the impact of Social Proof (and just a few words) can be with the story of Colleen Szot—one of the most successful writers in the paid programming industry. In addition to writing several very successful well-known "infomercials" for the immensely successful exercise machine, NordicTrack, she shattered records for a popular home shopping channel, literally shocking the ad industry by merely changing a few words to a standard spoken line.

Instead of the tag line, "Operators are waiting, please call now," she convinced network execs that saying "If operators are busy, please call again" would work better. At first glance, Szot's suggested wording sounded more like a pledge of bad service, discouraging callers by hinting they may waste their time on hold or redialing just to get an operator or someone to help. On the other hand, Szot considered the mental image conjured by "operators are waiting," that of dozens of bored phone reps, yawning, reading magazines, and hoping not to be interrupted with an occasional customer— low demand and poor sales.

Szot's phrasing said…if the lines are busy then "…other people who saw the same commercial I just saw are calling, too." In essence, Social Proof holds true even when the other people are not known or aren't similar to the customer.

In a 1969 study by scientist Stanley Milgram and others, published by the *Journal of Personality & Social Psychology*, when a worker stopped on a busy New York street and began staring at the sky for sixty seconds, hardly anyone reacted. However, when four others were added, the number of passersby who jumped in on the gazing more than quadrupled.

Of course, many people would deny that the actions of others influence them in this way. They are, after all, independent thinkers capable of making their own decisions (sarcasm intended). But, Goldstein and Martin proved the converse. For decades, the hotel industry posted signs in guest bathrooms encouraging guests to "reuse" their towels. The wording varied a little, but the pitch never did in appealing to a guest's concern for the environment. It never varied from one city to another, from one hotel chain to another. Always, guests were encouraged to reuse towels as a means to decrease the use of water, detergents, etc., and as a way to "do your small part" to protect the environment. Then, Goldstein and Martin, merely to test their theory of Social Proof, approached hotels to make slight changes to the "towel" signs and asked the cleaning staff to keep a record of who reused the towels and how often. After years of using the same, proven successful approach of appealing to a guest's sense of ecology, and after an unvarying campaign based on protecting the environment, they simply changed the phrasing to read "…a majority of other guests reuse their towels at least once a day."

After guests read the new wording, which had never been used in any hotel anywhere prior to that time, the guests were 26 percent more likely to recycle their towels. That's 26 percent higher than that industry's standard by simply changing a few words.

As you create General Benefit Statements for each of your points, or sub-points, think of the connection between your product/service and the prospect buyer. Think of ways to work a Social Proof into each of your points and sub-points. Think of each word. Show exactly how your product or service solves their specific problem by solving similar problems of others. Give real life examples, using the seller's business or personal experiences to enhance your points and draw parallels to other similar businesses. Examine each phrase of each benefit statement to make sure it conveys the appropriate message of Social Proof.

Step #5—Write out your concluding comments, including a summary of what you've told the audience, and request a commitment or some action or follow up on their part.
There is an old axiom that says, "…Tell them what you are going to tell them. Tell them, and then tell them what you told them." It's a good axiom.

The closing is your chance to reinforce the central theme and purpose of your presentation. You do this by "briefly" re-emphasizing the key benefits and main ideas of your product and presentation. In a well structured closing, points raised during the question and answer session (if any) are summarized and any handout material that was during the presentation is distributed. Handout material that emphasizes each key point or idea permits your audience to review the subject and assures that your words will remain fresh in their minds.

Check back with the buyers to assure that their presentation goals were met. "Did I cover all of the points you wanted to get from this presentation?" A questionnaire distributed at the end of your presentation can be a source of critical information for follow-up calls or future presentations. Encourage the attendants to call or write with any questions that they did not get answered during the presentation.

You need to always ask for something. Don't let the audience wonder what it is they are now supposed to go do. Whether you are asking for a "check" or are merely one presenter in a long line of competing presentations, it's important that some action, response, or commitment be requested. You might summarize your main points or you might complete the statement, "What I want you to do as a result of this presentation is..." But beyond that, make your last words a thought to ponder. Do not make it easy for your listeners to ignore and forget what you've been saying to them.

And, just like you started strong, end strong too: "...so that's why I'm proud to work for XYZ and I hope that soon I'll be working with you. Thank you." Then stand there and wait. Even small groups will often clap at this point because you just told them you were done. When they've finished, ask them if they have any questions. If nobody asks anything, break the uncomfortable silence with "Well, I guess I told you everything you need to know then. I'll be around after if you think of anything. Thanks again!" and start packing up your stuff.

After performing Steps #1 through #5 above, some would say that their presentation was fully prepared. And, for experienced presenters and smaller or less important presentations that may be all that's necessary. But, for those with larger audiences, perhaps a hundred or more, or those where the stakes are high or those with a lot of graphics or all of the above, there may be more work to be done.

Let's continue.

Step #6—Rehearse your presentation using a stop watch. Refine it accordingly. Rehearse it again.
I've never heard a presentation be as good as it could be until it was thoroughly rehearsed. I consider failure to rehearse to be the number one omission that could avoid most of the mediocre or down-

right "lousy" presentations I've witnessed. As the Royal Academy of Dramatic Arts (RADA) puts it "Professionals practice. Amateurs don't feel the need."

Just like a one-on-one sales call must be managed, so too must a group presentation. Rehearsing helps you manage the audience. Losing control of your audience shows a lack of proper planning. Pauses, misplaced papers, unclear explanations due to lack of rehearsal, all breed confusion and promote loss of control. Preparation is vital for success. Do you know how many will be in the audience? Adequate rehearsal is also a tool I use in the design and format of the proposal itself. Do you have enough seats, hard copies, samples, etc., for everyone? What is their current level of knowledge? How will you get their attention? How will you manage questions, as you go along or at the end? Where will you stand? Sure, if you're an experienced seller/presenter doing what you've done a thousand times, maybe there isn't a real need. But, if it's an important presentation, why take the chance?

Your final script and outline permit you to rehearse your presentation even before the visuals are completed. This assures that when your final images are prepared and ready you will be as well.

If you'd like to really test your mettle, drag out the video camera. If you do, be sure to stop it when you have to jot down a note about changing something. This helps the camcorder act similar to the stop watch. With the stop watch you rehearse and "stop" whenever you uncover something that needs to be changed, enhanced, or deleted. If you've stopped the watch appropriately, you'll have an accurate measure of how long your presentation is. One thing: always add about five minutes for every half-hour of your rehearsed time. In real life, questions, additional words, or a spontaneous story or comment usually adds considerable time and is why most "live" presentations run longer than rehearsed.

Step #7—Decide on graphics and put the first draft together using the graphics you will use.
The phrase "a picture is worth a thousand words" has existed since

the *New York Post* discovered the value of visuals in the news business 100 years ago. Since then, research has confirmed that people learn more readily and retain more information when learning is reinforced by visualization.

You can entertain, inform, excite, and even shock an audience by the proper integration of visual images into virtually any exchange of information. However, you must begin mentally planning your visuals at the beginning of the design process. Hastily designed and produced visuals can doom a presentation (and a presenter) where well planned and professionally executed images add tremendous strength. Concepts that are difficult to grasp can be communicated quickly and easily through the intelligent use of professionally produced visuals. This allows you the freedom to communicate more complex subject matter in a more efficient manner, adding support and impact to your points and sub-points.

Concise visual images peppered with simple, clear, attention-grabbing graphics will lend support to your spoken words and leave your audience with a positive attitude toward you and your product, service or proposal.

But, your visuals should be used in support of what you say, and not in lieu of it. A well-developed outline with effective points and sub-points is the essence of any presentation and the graphics are developed around them, not the other way around.

PowerPoint—Especially for formal presentations with large groups of 20 or more, I recommend preparing a PowerPoint computer slide presentation. In the future, there may be something better, but for right now, if done right, PowerPoint is hard to beat for larger groups. For smaller groups other options, like flip charts, handing out your outline, or the typical "packet" of information will often do if professionally prepared and free of errors.

Materials that accompany the presentation, with errors, either technical or typographical in nature, tell the audience they aren't important and you, your company or product, aren't organized or efficient. Proofread everything! Twice! Or, have someone else do it.

A five-minute presentation to a three person audience is probably best made with handout material alone or even simple flip charts. Sometimes slightly larger audiences might be effectively reached by using a few simple overhead transparencies; these have the advantage of enabling you to write on them while you speak to emphasize points or to jot down a question or point from the audience.

A PowerPoint presentation keeps you in control, enabling you to make certain you hit on all your key points. Preparing a Power-Point presentation is a good discipline for figuring out what you want to say even if you don't end up using the show itself. Be sure to place the buyers company logo on your slides and describe how the key slides relate to their situation.

If the previous steps have been carefully followed, this can be the easiest part of preparing your presentation. This is true whether you use Magic Markers to prepare flip charts or use Power Point.

Images not clearly seen by the entire audience add confusion and distraction. If you have to say "I know you can't read this, but...," why include the visual at all? Can you reduce it to two separate visuals? How about a handout? Whether accompanied with an apology or not, causing your audience or any part of your audience to strain to read a visual rarely motivates and often distracts entirely from the points you are trying to make.

You can use the "eight times rule." Essentially, if you can read an image at a distance that is eight times its height, odds are your audience will be able to read it when projected. As an example...you have a flip chart that is three feet high. If you can read the chart from 24 feet away, that chart will probably be legible when converted to a slide or overhead transparency or projected PowerPoint image.

While Googling for presentation visuals, I found much information on how to prepare effective visuals. There are many innovative ideas and technologies available and likely there'll be more in the future. I would suggest you spend some time researching what works best for you. Stephen Eggleston, for one example, is an acknowledged expert in Internet publishing, communications, user interface design, presentation graphics, photography, marketing, and knowledge management. He, among others I found, offered the following advice for your visuals:

The Useless Image—Images should be designed to please the mind as well as the eye of the viewer. If an image has no specific place or purpose in a presentation other than "it looks cool," drop it.

The Overly Complex Image—More images with fewer ideas on each are better than a few complicated or difficult to understand images. A single idea or set of facts per image, timed to the speaker's pace, will add punch and emphasis to each point and improve audience retention.

Most people are easily bored, and one generally accepted rule of thumb states that if an image remains on the screen longer than seven to ten seconds, you begin to lose viewer attention.

Chart Distractions—Chart distractions identify confusing elements, which really have no place on the image. Many presenters insist on having a glaring colored logo in the corner of every image. While a common element can add continuity to a presentation, blinking logos or other distractions often only detract from the message.

Chart Playfulness—Don't try to be too cute. Sometimes graphic images are overly cute attempts to make a presentation appear more professional by adding lots of distracting, tacky, aggravating symbols, and such. These usually appear right after a presenter has discovered a clip art library.

Colors & Font—Just because you have access to 35 fonts does not mean that you are required to use them. A single font throughout an entire presentation is usually quite sufficient. Use bold, italic, underline, quotations, and/or color changes to emphasize or subdue key points or words.

Keep the colors to a minimum. A single background color throughout a presentation lends an air of continuity. You can separate broad sections of a presentation by changing background colors, but keep the changes to a minimum. Unless your purpose is to shock or grab serious attention, try to keep all background colors within the same color family.

Mixed Visual Metaphors—Just like when you speak, you should avoid mixing metaphors with your graphics. Try to have your images align with the points you are making as to color, shape, size, and other characteristics.

Seek the Experts—When it come to visuals, the Internet is a wonderful playground. There are even private vendors who will take the outline of your presentation and, for a fee, convert it to dazzling computer graphics. The entire arrangement with such vendors can be procured online and with little hassle. Give it a shot, but remember…the only one who knows what will work for your audience and your purpose…is you.

Step #8—Using a stop watch, rehearse your presentation again, using the visuals and in front of a live audience of friends, co-workers, or family members. Focus on your manner, presentation style, and delivery.
There isn't anything you do or say while presenting that can't be rehearsed in front of an audience of your peers. Your movements, your words, your facial expressions, your hand movements are all open to being improved with practice. I understand that a seller of a product is not necessarily in need of becoming a professional speaker or a stand up comedian. However, for those who care or for those who want to be the best presenter they can be, spending some time on your delivery can be quite beneficial.

Again, you can find all sorts of professional speakers who have valuable advice and have shared their experience on the Internet. I've searched and come up with what seems to me to be some key elements that I practice myself and/or observe in others more successful than I. The bibliography includes some of the sites I visited to develop this list.

Stand away from the podium, out from behind the presenter's table. Keep your hands out of your pockets. I pace a little bit around the stage or the boardroom, timed with my points, saying one thing from over here and another from over there. But don't move too much and engage in what's called "nervous pacing."

Pause when you say something important. Let it hang there for a few seconds. Try it when talking to your friends. "You know what I think?" (Pause...two...three...four...) and then tell them.

Be animated. The majority of sales presentations I have heard have been boring and unimaginative. If you really want to stand out from the crowd, make sure you demonstrate enthusiasm and energy. Vary your modulation, your tempo, your volume. A common mistake made when people talk about a product with which they are very familiar is to allow that familiarity to manifest itself in a monotonous speech pattern or a rapid fire delivery.

If you videotape your rehearsals or presentations, it will allow you to hear exactly what you sound like; I highly recommend it.

Have answers prepared. As you prepare your presentation, anticipate as many possible questions and have clear concise answers ready. That way, you won't be flustered. "I'm glad you asked that," or "Great question," you can reply, and then launch into your prepared response. Always repeat the question for larger audiences.

Deliver; don't read. An outline is appropriate to help you stay on point. Reading your presentation, however, is downright boring and reduces your credibility. Never do it.

Act like a professional. Your body language counts, too. Maintain an "up" posture; use open hand gestures (with elbows away from the body), look directly at your audience, and show them (through facial expressions, voice, energy) that you feel confident and positive.

A limited use of humor is okay. Don't panic at this suggestion; you are not becoming a comedian, but rather lightening up a serious speech so that people will be more accepting and interested in your ideas.

But, until you have lots of experience, or unless you are giving a humorous keynote presentation, keep your humor short. Perhaps inject a one-liner or a quotation. Yogi Berra said a lot of funny things. "You can observe a lot just by watching," for example. Tell a short embarrassing moment from your life that you might have thought not funny at the time. Now that you can laugh at the experience, you understand the old adage, "Humor is simply tragedy separated by time and space." Never tell long stories or jokes when making a sales presentation.

Make eye contact. If it is a small audience, you can look at everyone many times. If it is a large audience, look at them in sections and move from one to another. One way to insure good eye contact is to look at your audience before you start to speak. Go to the lectern and pause, smile, look at one-third, then another third, and then begin speaking while looking at the final third. This will help you maintain good eye contact throughout your presentation as well as commanding immediate attention.

Dealing with nerves. Nervousness, speech anxiety, stage fright, platform panic—it's known by many names, but it's a problem every speaker must confront. Actually, feeling nervous before a speech is healthy. It shows that your speech is important to you and that you care about doing well. But unless you can manage and control your nervousness, it can keep you from becoming an effective speaker.

I promise that if you follow the steps suggested here, in particular those dealing with rehearsing, you will have done all you can do to minimize the impact of "nerves."

Recognize you're not alone and that people want you to succeed. Have you ever watched a comedian bomb? It is, without a doubt, one of the most difficult things to witness, primarily because we put ourselves in their shoes and feel sorry for them. We listen to jokes that don't make us laugh and we laugh because we don't want them to fail. Every audience you present to, even if they aren't inspired by your product, will still want you to deliver a quality presentation. Keep this in mind, but...never start by telling them you are inexperienced at presenting or by asking for their sympathy and understanding if you make a mistake or two. This only tells them to keep an eye out for anything that might be the mistake you told them to watch out for. Act professional and your audience will most likely think you are.

Experience builds confidence—your anxieties decrease the more presentations you give. That's the point of rehearsing. If you are still nervous maybe you need to rehearse more.

After thorough rehearsal, the need for highly detailed notes should be removed. However, there may be a need sometimes to have the "security blanket" of a few key notes, perhaps highlighted on small prompt cards. The key thing here to remember is that notes should be used to support the presentation and not replace it or get in the way of you delivering with impact.

Step #9—Revise based on any constructive criticism from #8.
Make it a preparation goal to collate all the presentation material, slides, handouts etc., at least 48 hours before the presentation time. Then spend the remaining 48 hours rehearsing and concentrating on how you are going to present rather than what you are going to present...remember, you are the presentation not your material.

By following all the above tips you should be in a highly confident and positive frame of mind. This will naturally come across to your audience, who will develop a stake in seeing you succeed. The more you follow the above rules, the easier it will become to draft and deliver future presentations. It may not always be necessary or appropriate to do every step every time, at least not formally. But, having the habit of considering each step, at least mentally, is a good sign you have reached Elite Status with respect to group presentations.

Good Luck!

PLATFORM III

Self Management

PLATFORMS OF SUCCESS

Chapter 18

THE ELITE MANAGEMENT OF TIME

*When I'm working on a problem, I never think about beauty.
I think only of how to solve the problem; but when I'm
finished, if the solution isn't beautiful, I know it is
wrong...Buckminster Fuller*

A portion of every sales class I taught and one of the more popular training seminars I used to conduct for convention or management programs deals with the subject typically known as Time Management—the idea that goal setting, planning, organizing, and prioritizing one's daily activities, can increase production and success among other things. I subscribe to the theory wholeheartedly and that's why Platform III deals with Self and Time Management.

At the micro level (the level of day-to-day activities), as long as your tasks relate to the achievement of properly set goals, effectiveness can be measured merely by the "timely" completion of those tasks. Properly setting sales goals, those that achieve your personal revenue goals, then making sure those daily activities relate to the goals is the macro level—the sum total of the two is Self Management.

At the beginning of Platform II, I said I could've been more successful at selling if I had merely avoided making mistakes and that I could've made better group presentations if the only thing I did

165

different was avoid a few obvious faux pas I observed in presentations given by others. Likewise, it is true that I could've been more productive no matter what I was doing—whether selling, presenting, teaching, or managing—not so much with the luxury of more time (though that would've been nice), but merely by managing better the time I had been given.

Being talented will never overcome being bad at managing the details of your life or the details of your life's work. Being on time, being organized, being responsible with the little time you have been blessed with, for both personal and professional endeavors, is an irreplaceable cornerstone of successful selling and can often overcome a non-competitive product or poor delivery. Coincidentally, poor Self Management is the single greatest reason for mediocrity and failure in the business world.

The Fuller Factor
Maybe you took note of the quotation beneath the title of this chapter referencing solutions that are "beautiful." Many years ago while I was serving as president of the Florida Society of Association Executives (FSAE), I was captivated by a presentation from a man who was one of Walt Disney's closest confidantes and who later parlayed that relationship into a successful speaking and consulting business. His talk impressed me so much that I began referencing parts of it in my classes on Time Management. The speaker's name was Mike Vance and, shortly after hearing his presentation, I began calling the development of so called "beautiful" solutions as The Fuller Factor.

Mike spoke of the time when Walt Disney directed him to come up with ways that Disneyland could increase its revenues. My recollection is that he had to do so without developing new products or investing in new capital intensive ventures—"quite a challenge for one of the most successful and profitable businesses in the world," Vance must have thought.

Mike shared Walt Disney's penchant for Time Management and of getting the most out of every minute. He knew also of Disney's

166

unique approach to brainstorming and creativity. Indeed, the phrase, "Think out of the box," actually developed as a way to describe Disney's unique approach to problem solving. It was Mike's task, or so he thought, to incorporate Walt Disney's respect for time and approach to creativity into an overall plan to increase profitability, but...nothing was coming to mind; nothing, that is, until Mike and Walt had dinner with the inventor of the geodesic dome, an architect and author named Buckminster Fuller.

Fuller's book, *Nine Chains to the Moon*, referred to the fact that if the population of humans were to stand one on top of each other, they would form chains that could reach back and forth to the moon nine times. In it he overviewed technological world history and a vision of the future driven by "ephemeralization;" a term he coined, referencing the doing of more with less. Fuller often used Henry Ford's assembly line as the perfect example of a beautiful solution—fewer people, less plant and equipment, but...more output and productivity. That evening's dinner conversation must have been stimulating beyond imagination. Mike Vance, Walt Disney, and a world famous visionary, sharing ideas and their views on corporate productivity.

Vance was impressed enough, the story goes, to gather a team of Disney's "out of the box" thinkers, lock them in a room, and tell them of Walt's challenge and, perhaps, Fuller's theories. They began by doing something I later implemented in my company. I called it time logging. In Disney's case, they simply examined how Disneyland was currently using its hours.

Since there was no need to waste time and money when no one was going to come to the park, Disneyland, at the time, was closed every Monday and Tuesday. And, on Wednesdays, Thursdays, and Saturdays it was only open for half a day. Mike's out of the box creative team saw opportunity to employ The Fuller Factor; how could they get more revenue when the park was currently closed?

They started by simply thumbing through the yellow pages to spark idea's. When they got to the "Cs," lights went on! "What if we formed a club?" someone asked. And, thus was born the Magic Kingdom Club, which attracted enough attention to keep the parks open on every weekday.

Eventually, the idea of offering the park to high schools came about. Teenagers, they figured, liked clubs and would enjoy the late hours and preferential treatment; and thus was born the Disney tradition of "Grad Night."

It all worked to produce more revenue and profitability from the same 24 hours—a "beautiful" solution.

The Pennsylvania Problem
The Fuller Factor came to roost years later when my company's sales began to sag horribly, particularly in the state of Pennsylvania as the result of a well-funded, locally-imbedded competitor with a far less expensive product. While price was an Objection we were experts at overcoming, this competitor also employed sellers who were former insurance agents with specific knowledge about rating (pricing) insurance policies. They were killing us with sales presentations reflecting the nuances of insurance rating scenarios tailored not only to property and casualty agents but specifically to problems in the state of Pennsylvania. It was an inside track we couldn't seem to overcome. I was discouraged from months of trying to find a solution, and the pressure from "upstairs" was increasing.

Meanwhile, and unrelated to the Pennsylvania problem, I had a lunch interview with a sales recruit from Allentown named Frank. His résumé didn't hold the solutions I was looking for. While his lack of knowledge about our product (an automated insurance policy rating system) could be overcome with a few weeks training, he didn't know the basic concepts of how to rate an insurance policy either—a distinct disadvantage when selling against our new competitor. Still, Frank looked the part and there was a sense of urgency in his manner and voice that caught my fancy. He was aggressive and let it be known that he was willing to do what was necessary to get the job. He took notes during the interview. He looked me in the eye. He smiled, laughed, and spoke at all the right times. He asked the right questions. And…he listened, took notes, and responded to my answers.

Nonetheless, our training investment (up-front compensation and monthly draw package) in each seller was substantial enough that we couldn't take chances. Rarely did we hire someone based on "gut" instincts.

Honestly, had I been in Frank's shoes, interviewing for a job knowing I lacked the basic experience requirements, I might have tried to impress my interviewer with enthusiasm for learning whatever needed to be learned in order to do, and to get, the job. Frank, of course, said he would learn whatever was necessary, but he showed little enthusiasm in this regard and even said he didn't think it was imperative he do so in order to succeed. Say what? "You don't think it's important?" I asked in complete disbelief.

As I persisted, stressing the importance of learning the fundamentals of insurance policy rating, I told Frank that not having the prerequisite requirement was like a death sentence in selling my company's software system. I was thinking…"how can you help me solve my Pennsylvania problem?"

I asked him, "How can you answer even the basic questions that will surely come your way? How will you explain how the various functions of the system will deal with this, that, or the other scenario in rating a complicated Commercial General Liability Insurance policy?" Frank didn't even know what I was talking about, but his response was always the same.

"Mr. Johnson, having the knowledge you speak of will come in time, but until it does, selling your product will be just a numbers game for me. Whatever I lack in product knowledge in the beginning will be made up with more calls on more prospects. Later, when I have the knowledge you say is so important, I'll be the best in your company; for right now, because I'll work harder and smarter, my numbers will still be as good as the rest."

When I looked across the table at an organized, neat, confident, note taker and heard that comment, I was flustered to say the least. But...as I pondered what to do, I remembered The Fuller Factor—attacking convention, being creative, taking chances, and developing beautiful solutions. So, after much thought and introspection, I took a chance by giving Frank a chance. And, it made all the difference.

Without the technical experience to meet our monthly closing requirements, Frank went about things much like the team at Disney—with some out of the box thinking. Instead of calling on prospects one at a time, spending several hours being grilled by an expert at rating insurance policies and then moving on to the next office where the same thing would take place perhaps a total of three times a day (if you were lucky), he designed a brochure from the company training materials and invited six to ten decision makers to his hotel room or the hotel's business center for what he called "continuing education." He also promised to teach them how to beat the competition with our system. He asked his "students" to bring their "unrated" policies with them. He asked one of them to rate an insurance policy using our company's automated system while the others watched. Present in the room was an existing satisfied user who could answer questions, even demo the system, and who doubled as a Social Proof source when anyone expressed Skepticism about a feature, our company's reputation, or the service contract.

Frank contacted almost three times as many prospects as the rest of the sales team. His first month in the field, despite having the least populous territory, he topped my two other Pennsylvania reps by nearly 20 percent. The second month, he was the top seller again, but this time for the entire country. During our next sales meeting, Frank showed everyone how to set up and conduct the demonstrations. Soon, all of my sellers were doing the same thing in each of their territories. And, it wasn't long before my Pennsylvania problem was solved, unit sales were through the roof, and...I began to understand that it wasn't necessary for me to labor so much trying to recruit only former insurance producers. I began looking for those who were truly out-of-the-box sellers…like Frank.

And Frank? Well, he remained the top seller until he was hired away by our competition, which had grown tired of losing against his aggressive creativity. But, his ideas became part of our basic sales repertoire and accounted for hundreds of sales we would not have otherwise made. Today I'm convinced the seller I almost didn't hire is the president of a company that probably wouldn't hire me. I may have been the teacher, but I learned more from that one student than I had from any book or from any videotaped role-plays.

The point in mentioning The Fuller Factor is that selling skills, and managing one's time are as important to success as taking chances, being creative, and thinking out of the box. Whenever, you're tapped out or think you can go no further; whenever you feel you can't produce any better, sell any more, achieve anything higher; remember the yellow pages, remember Frank and remember The Fuller Factor—there's always a beautiful solution out there somewhere.

Las Vegas Engineering
Most of what I learned about the micro-level of Time Management came from my friend and perhaps unwitting mentor, Dr. John Lee of "Time, Life & Lee." Dr. Lee was a management professor at Florida State University who often spoke on the subject of Time Management. At one point my company procured his services to advise on what we could do to make our staff and our sellers more productive. He had a concept for the micro level that was like The Fuller Factor was to the macro level—an overriding concept that can make all the difference in your success or failure.

John Lee called the concept Las Vegas Engineering, referring to Vegas casinos who were experts at "creating the conditions for success; their own success."

Think about every casino you've ever been in. Why are there no windows? Why are there no clocks? Why is the temperature on the cool side? Why do rumors persist that casinos pump oxygen into the duct system?

Have you ever been to a for-profit establishment anywhere in the world where you drink (and often eat) for free? Have you ever known of any other establishment where you convert your money to plastic, in part, so you don't feel quite so bad when you leave it all behind?

My favorite is when casinos began displaying lighted signs showing how many times the roulette wheel had come up either red or black. It would show seven successive blacks and everyone would rush the table to vote on red. If the sign showed a large number of successive reds, a crowd would gather to vote on black at the next turn of the wheel.

The casino's knew that no matter how many times the wheel came up black (or red), the odds never changed. The chances that a coin will come up heads or tails is always 50/50 regardless of how many times in a row it comes up one or the other. And, like the toss of a coin, past spins of the roulette wheel don't alter the odds of the current spin.

In Vegas, wherever there's a line, there are slot machines—at hotel check in counters, in the airport, at the rental car agencies, at restaurants, waiting to get in a show. Token after token, millions upon millions of "fake" money is poured into machines 24 hours a day, 365 days a year—by college kids, blue collar workers, people on welfare, and wide eyed soccer moms all looking for a cheap (or rather expensive) thrill by engaging in the most prolific money wasting effort on planet earth…that's Las Vegas Engineering.

Creating Conditions For Success
The point of looking at how Las Vegas engineers its success is to illustrate that we can engineer our lives similarly. And, to illustrate that we often do the opposite, engineering large portions of our lives to maximize failure.

Take a look at one of the first acts we humans perform each day of our adult lives—certainly each working day—the ritualistic setting of an alarm clock. At night, every night, millions of us decide what time we need to get up in the morning. Before we pull the covers up, we either set the clock, or confirm that it's still set, for that time. We have various options. We can choose the length and number of each snooze, music or buzzer, volume level, etc.—all choices that customize the same function to an individual user without sacrificing the main goal: that of getting us out of bed in the morning.

Let me say that again, the main goal of using an alarm clock is what? To get us out of the bed in the morning! Yet, in my seminars on Time Management, if I asked a room of 100 sellers who use an alarm clock where they locate that clock in their bedroom, virtually all of them gave the same answer: "On the nightstand next to my bed."

"And why do you put your alarm clock next to your bed?" I asked.

"So I don't have to get out of bed to turn it off," they inevitably responded.

You see, the opposite of Las Vegas Engineering is present in most of our lives and it starts with the very first act we perform every morning and the last one we perform every night. In between the setting and stopping of our alarm, our work environment, our habits, our organization of activities are also often structured to maximize the chances of failure.

To learn the techniques for the Elite Management of Time, we must first put some Las Vegas Engineering into our daily routine. Like the casinos in Las Vegas and like everything else, it all starts with the setting of goals because goals that are not properly established are infinitely more difficult to obtain, assuming they were goals in the first place.

Indeed, all of Time Management and Self Management (and the next two chapters) fall into two areas of equal importance and difficulty—one, setting goals; and two, reaching the goals you've set.

173

Chapter 19

STARTING WITH GOALS
*The greater danger for most of us is not that our aim
is too high and we miss it, but that it is too low and we
reach it—Michelangelo*

In Lewis Caroll's timeless short story, *Alice's Adventures In Wonderland*, Alice's path is crossed by a nervous rabbit frantically late for an appointment. "Oh dear, oh dear, I shall be late!" the Rabbit exclaims.

A talking rabbit in a waistcoat, a first certainly, but Alice's Rabbit also had a watch. Curious, she chased after it, down the rabbit hole that began her famous journey through wonderland. Alice's adventure is much like a day in the life of someone without goals, or with poorly drawn goals—much time is wasted just chasing rabbits... rabbits with watches!

The parallel comes more into focus when Alice arrives at a fork—the point where she must make a choice; which direction to head, which road to take? A nearby Cheshire Cat seems quite knowledgeable about such things, so she begs for assistance.

"... would you tell me which way I ought to go from here?"

"That depends a great deal on where you want to get to" said the cat.

"I don't much care where" said Alice.

"Then it doesn't matter which way you go..."

In essence, the decisions we make and the activities we perform each day only have relevance when juxtaposed with a destination, a goal; everything else is just chasing rabbits down a hole...rabbits with watches!

The Time Perspective

Harvard Professor Dr. Edward Banfield spent years researching the personal characteristics that promote upward mobility in society. He wanted to know why some people moved up, earned more, achieved their dreams, or succeeded, while others did not. After years of testing various hypotheses, he finally concluded that it was largely due to differing time perspectives.

Banfield found that those who became successful invariably had a longer time perspective. They took the future into consideration when they planned their daily, weekly, and monthly activities. They thought five, ten, and twenty years down the road. They allocated their resources and made their decisions based on how their choices would affect where they wanted to be several years hence.

Conversely, according to Banfield, less successful people had shorter time perspectives. They gave less thought to the long-term or were more concerned with immediate gratification than end results; they were more concerned with having fun today or tonight than with enjoying financial security or success tomorrow or the next day. This attitude towards time, or time perspective, made them endure longer-term hardships in exchange for shorter-term gratification.

In 1953, a questionnaire was circulated to the graduating seniors at Yale University. They were asked the question, "Do you have clear, specific, written goals for your life, and have you developed complete plans for their accomplishment after you leave this university?"

The results would be surprising for any university, but were startling for graduating seniors at one of America's most prestigious institutions of higher learning. Only three percent of Yale's graduating class had clear written goals and plans for what they wanted to do after graduation. Thirteen percent had goals, but had not written them down. The other 84 percent had no goals at all except to enjoy the summer or spend some time relaxing before they developed them, sought gainful employment, or began a career.

Twenty years later, in 1973, the surviving members of that same Yale class were surveyed again. Among other questions, they were asked about their net worth. When the results were averaged, the three percent who had clear, written goals at graduation twenty years earlier were worth more in dollar terms than the entire remaining 97 percent of the class.

There were no other consistently identifiable factors linking the former students. Some had previously made good grades, some had poorer grades. Some worked in one industry, some in another. Some had moved many times or across the country or job hopped, and some had stayed put. Clearly defined, written goals was the only thing the top performers had in common—their common denominator was intense goal-orientation from the very beginning.

The story goes that the Yale grads who set goals and implemented their plans also had more fulfilling, happier personal lives as well. Logically, when you are working towards something that is important to you, each step is fulfilling because you are moving ahead to something you want. You feel more in control of your life. And, because you feel more successful and thus relevant, you develop a psychological momentum that enables you to push past adversity. Those without clearly defined, written goals are often unfulfilled or less content even when through chance, talent, or hard work they may experience some measure of achievement.

With the idea in mind that work-related goals are not independent, but, indeed, are indelibly tied to your personal goals and happiness, over the next several pages I'm going to spend considerable time helping you develop a longer-term perspective for your life for both professional and domestic goals.

Effective Goals

Some people have goals for virtually every part of their life—a concept with which I have no problem—one set of goals for work; one for hobbies and recreational activities, like golf or tennis, for example; and a separate set for family, volunteer activities, or personal investments, and more. Some people have goals they are always updating, deleting, meeting, or…failing to meet.

What is lost on these so called "goal oriented" people is that "the goal" isn't to have goals; it is to "achieve" goals. And, that means the activity of "goal setting" is as important as having goals in the first place. In fact, the only thing worse than not having any goals is having only those that are poorly drafted. This is true regardless of which area of life a goal applies. The rules are always the same.

To be more than just a fun exercise, to be truly effective, sales goals and objectives (any goal or objective) must hold up against eight specific criteria. If they do not, most likely they aren't goals; they are dreams or wishes. Don't misunderstand…wishes, dreams, fantasies, and the like are helpful motivational tools and often necessary for overachieving. This lesson, however, isn't about wishes and dreams; it's about achieving the sales goals necessary to fulfill those wishes and dreams.

To be effective, a properly set goal must meet all eight of the following characteristics. It must:

1.) **Be Specific**—A goal or an objective must be calculable and finite. A goal stated along the lines of "Be a better manager" lacks definition and can be achieved based on subjective opinions that can vary from one person to another.

2.) **Be Measurable**—There must be a criteria for determining the extent to which you are moving toward or have achieved the goal or objective.

3.) **Be Attainable**—If you can't reach a goal under reasonable circumstances, it may be motivational or comforting (or frustrating) to have such; it may be a dream or a wish, but...it's not a goal or an objective that is helpful to successful selling. Too many unattainable goals may also yield a lifetime of unhappiness.

4.) **Be Time Bound**—There must be a point in time when you know you have either achieved the goal or objective, usually defined as success, or you have not achieved it, sometimes defined as failure. Don't be afraid of either one.

5.) **Be Meaningful**—Don't set goals that are too easily achieved or select goals that have already been achieved or nearly so. By setting goals or objectives that you were on the verge of achieving anyway you not only waste time but you give yourself the false sense of accomplishment that enables you to keep on failing without consequence.

6.) **Be Controllable**—Goals must be within your ability to achieve and not left to events that you cannot control.

7.) **Be Written**—Reduce your goals and objectives to writing. Something that exists only in your mind doesn't really exist. Keep written goals in a highly visible place. Review your written goals regularly to keep focus or to occasionally revise when necessary and appropriate.

8.) **Be Communicated To Relevant Others**—This is the most often forgotten rule and is the embodiment of Las Vegas Engineering; those who don't tell others their goals are trying to avoid embarrassment if they fail; that just increases the chances that they will fail.

Write It Down; Pass It Around

You'll notice that numbers seven and eight are a bit different from numbers one through six. Seven and eight are things you do with the goal once it is established; you write it down and then communicate it to others. One through six are what the goal should look like or how it should be structured, which, were it not for numbers seven and eight, could've all been done in your head. Indeed, many people have goals that exist merely in their heads.

Amway Corporation provides the following for its sales personnel:

> One final tip before you get started: Set a goal and write it down. Whatever the goal, the important thing is that you set it, so you've got something for which to aim—and that you write it down. There is something magical about writing things down. So set a goal and write it down. When you reach that goal, set another and write that down. You'll be off and running.

If Amway's instructions sound like motivational fluff to you, consider the words of three experts, Cialdini, Goldstein, and Martin who said; "commitments that are made actively have more staying power than those that are made passively," and who proved it with a study by social scientists Delia Cioffi and Randy Gardner.

Cioffi and Gardner proved the power of written goals with an experiment using volunteers for an education project. Students were given two sets of instructions, active and passive. The active instructions said that if you wanted to volunteer, fill out the form affirmatively, stating that you are willing to participate.

Those with the passive instructions were told that if they wanted to volunteer, they should not complete the form, saying they "didn't" want to participate. In summary: two forms, one to volunteer, one to decline. Two sets of people, those who were told to volunteer by filling out a form and those who were told to volunteer by not filling out a form.

Guess what? The number of people who volunteered didn't vary based on which way they were told to go, active (fill out a form) or passive (don't fill out a form). But...those who showed up to participate was dramatically different. Only 17 percent of the passive volunteers showed up. But, about two and a half times more of the active volunteers showed, participated, and kept their promises.

In retail stores, studies have proven that customers who fill out their own lay-away-forms are more likely to complete their payments vs. those where the salesperson completed the form for them. Keep this in mind when selling anything that requires form completion and a commitment from the buyer. But, more importantly…write down your own goals and communicate them to others!

Unlike personal goals, setting sales goals is usually an "objective" exercise based on measurements and other data unique to a particular industry or product. Often industry trade groups will provide the information necessary to determine the "average" cost of a sales call, the number of calls that are necessary to achieve an appointment, or the number of appointments or face to face meetings needed to close a sale, for example. An individual seller's ratio of appointments to closings is relevant to goal setting as is the industry or company data on the average number of phone calls (e-mails, contacts, etc.) needed to make an appointment.

A Life Plan
Having a goal in the future gives us direction for the present. Some individuals will have life goals referred to as Personal Mission Statements. There are two types of Personal Mission Statements: Domestic and Professional. It is appropriate to first spend some time contemplating how you want to "grow" as a human being, how you want to conduct yourself in relation to the world around you, and what kind of person you want to be when your life's work comes to a close. This can involve your life's work, the ultimate contribution you wish to make to humankind, and what kind of person (domestic) and seller (professional) you wish to become. When assembled with a strategy for accomplishing the mission, and personal and domestic revenue goals, you can develop an entire Life Plan.

In a corporate or business environment such statements are called Professional Mission Statements and apply to the relationship you wish to have with clients or other business constituents. When applied to your personal life, a Mission Statement is called a Domestic Mission Statement.

A typical **Domestic Mission Statement** could be:

To become known in my community as a kind, fair, hardworking, productive member of society and to become a sincere, loving, kind parent and spouse, who displays compassion and understanding to family members, close friends, and neighbors. To conduct all relationships by displaying the qualities of understanding, patience, and tolerance in order to be liked, respected, and admired by the people I meet and know and who know me.

A typical **Professional Mission Statement** could be:

To become known as the consummate professional seller in my field. To be knowledgeable about my products and services so that I can provide all buyers with a high quality affordable solution to their problems and needs. To be known as a person of the highest ethical standards who will always be prepared, dependable, punctual, compassionate, and understanding. To be, trusted, well liked, and admired by every client and prospect of my company.

Strategies

Some will recognize that within an overall mission there is often a basic strategy. This strategy often implements the overall financial goal of a company and often focuses on the particular "niche" of a business or of a seller as he/she moves forward with a career. For example, a business may decide to achieve its goals by focusing on selling to corporations of a particular type located in a particular geographic area, etc. An individual may want to become independently wealthy (within his/her personal definition of such) by a certain age (called a Domestic Financial Goal) by selling insurance, real estate, or widgets for XYZ Company, Inc. (a Strategy).

Corporate Mission Statements

You may already be familiar with a Corporate Mission Statement. For a business, these mission statements are often public documents that are displayed in corporate lobbies, appear in annual reports or even in sales materials, or on the actual product or its accompanying material. It is the organizational mantra and, as such, it should reflect a team consensus, employee buy-in, and scrutiny from legal authorities.

Domestic Financial Goals

Missions and strategies help businesses and individuals set their lifetime stage. And, while Platform III isn't primarily about the setting of that stage, I would encourage you to analyze your domestic goals and finances to see if your work-related sales goals are consistent. Developing an appropriate time perspective cannot be done if you are only considering one piece of your life to the exclusion of all others.

For example, analyzing the financial cost of maintaining and owning certain personal possessions, such as an expensive car or home, is often helpful when setting longer term annual sales goals or objectives. Before you set personal revenue goals at work (which will be broken down into manageable short-term objectives and which, in turn, can be reduced to daily work activities), you must first determine what achieving these goals will give you domestically or personally and whether or not that is enough for your long- and short-term happiness. This is part of establishing what I call your **Domestic Financial Goal**. You could have the goal to retire by a certain age and to have a specified amount of spendable cash when you do. If this is your long-term Domestic Financial Goal, you must set about establishing a plan for how you are going to achieve it, in part by reducing it to annual, quarterly, and/or monthly goals or objectives.

A Personal Prospectus

In developing your own Domestic Financial Goal, it's often helpful to take a look at your current and past financial progress. Pretend you're putting together a prospectus on yourself, much the way a corporation would do if it was conducting an IPO or looking for capital to finance a new venture. In this case, you start by determining your personal net worth.

Determining your net worth is easy. Maybe you can do it in your head, or get close enough, without using a calculator or pen and paper. Merely subtract everything you owe from everything you own. The difference is what you're worth.

Now, take that number, your net worth expressed in dollar terms, and divide it by the number of years you've been working. That's your average annual profit. If you've been working for 10 years and have a net worth of $100,000, then your average annual profit, or retained earnings, contribution to surplus, owners equity—whatever name you prefer to call it…is $10,000.

Figuring around 250 working days a year, this means you're averaging about $40 per day after expenses. Is this a good investment for your life? Will having this amount of money left over each day ($40), each year ($10,000), enable you to achieve your Domestic Financial Goal? Conducting this analysis is the only way to know. It's the only way to know whether your spending habits need to change in relation to your expected sales and take home revenues.

I know money can't buy happiness, but if you get paid to sell it's certainly important to make sure you can buy what you want with what you get paid. If you cannot, either your sales goals are too low or your domestic lifestyle is too high—a prescription for a lifetime of unhappiness. Around 70 percent of Americans have no discretionary income. Most spend more than what they make by about 10 percent, getting the deficit made up by loans, credit cards, and cash advances from guardians, parents, or friends. Live smart. Develop a long-term time perspective. Determine a Domestic Financial Goal and measure your progress towards that goal on an annual basis.

Self Management Chart
Now, this may all be getting a bit complicated, and it's likely you're saying, "Wow, there's more planning and analysis here than do-

ing." Actually, it's not as difficult as it sounds the first time you hear it and it isn't required that you do everything exactly as I've outlined. It is, however, an important part of success to have a well thought out plan that is properly designed and methodically executed and that takes into account each aspect of your life, domestic and professional.

To simplify, you may want to look at a sample of an overall Self Management Chart you could use in developing your own Life Plan; one follows a few pages forward. You may want to involve your spouse or significant other in your thought processes to help develop some buy-in. It's often helpful for him/her to understand that some extra time at work may mean some extra time at home later—earlier retirement, longer vacations, Fridays off. Either way, it wouldn't hurt to just attempt to complete a Self Management Chart as a way to acquaint yourself with what it is you really want to achieve in life and what you're willing to give up in order to achieve it. However…

…it's important to finish reading this chapter for some of the important formulas necessary in completing the charts, setting goals, and assembling a lifetime plan. Keep reading!

Personal Revenue Goals
Once you've established your Domestic Goals, you will have to set your personal revenue goals at work. There are no easy ways around it. No short cuts. No excuses. Elite Sellers establish long-term sales goals, usually annual ones. They then break them down into shorter-term objectives, which could be quarterly, monthly, or both, and sometimes weekly, depending on various factors. These objectives are then reduced to daily activities.

To establish your daily activities, you must first set your objectives related to prospects, which involves certain steps that could vary depending on your industry or product. And you must have some idea of both your Closing Ratio and the Average Revenue per Sale. A Closing Ratio is the likelihood of convincing a prospect to buy your product or service. Proficiencies developed from Platform I should help increase your Closing Ratio, as would techniques in developing prospects who are more qualified. Is your Closing Ratio 50 percent? In other words do you close half of the sales calls you make? Is it 20 percent? Do you close only one in five?

The Average Revenue per Sale is the average revenue you, or your peers, bring in with each sale. It's the mathematical result of dividing the number of sales calls by the total revenue from all sales made during the same period, usually over twelve months. For example, if all the sellers for your company made 100 sales calls last year and produced $1 million in revenue from those sales calls, then the Average Revenue per Sale is $10,000 (1,000,000/100) for the entire company.

Again, that's for the entire company. Your personal average is likely to be different, hopefully higher, than the company's average. It could also be that you made fewer sales calls than the average made by other sellers, but you made up for it with a higher Average Revenue per Sale or a better Closing Ratio or both. These are all terms Elite Sellers use and understand, and therefore ones that you should become familiar with regardless of what product you sell or for whom you sell it.

To develop a Personal Revenue Goal, perform the following steps:

1.) Find out what your average revenue per sale was last year using the above method or use an average developed by your employer or industry for sellers with similar experience. We'll assume $1,000.

2.) Find out what your Closing Ratio was last year, or develop a Closing Ratio that is reasonable for a new seller in your industry or company. We'll assume 50 percent.

3.) Use your properly set Domestic Financial Goals to determine the revenue figure you need to earn at work annually. We'll assume $100,000.

Personal Revenue Goal: $100,000
Quarterly Objectives: $25,000 average per quarter
Annual Sales Needed: 100 (if $1,000 average earnings per sale)

4,)   Determine your daily activities. Using the numbers above, your calculations should look something like this:

If 100 sales are needed over the course of 250 workdays per year, you will need to close two sales every week, or one sale every 2.5 days.

250/100 working days = 1 sale every 2.5 working days.
100 sales per year @ 50% closing ratio = 200 sales attempts needed.

Then, by simply increasing the percentage of prospects that result in sales, you can significantly increase your earnings. For example, let's say you met your income goal of $100,000 in your first year by closing 100 of 200 sales attempts. If, in the following year, you made the same amount of sales attempts (200), but by utilizing the skills from Platform I you increased your Closing Ratio to 60 percent, you would increase your income by 20 percent. It would look like this:

Year 1: 50% conversion (Closing Ratio) x 200 sales attempts = 100 sales
$100,000 annual income

Year 2: 60% conversion (Closing Ratio) x 200 sales attempts = 120 sales
$120,000 annual income

It's important to mention that figures such as the Average Revenue per Sale, or your Closing Ratio (conversion rate) can vary dramatically from one industry to another, and sometimes from one year to another, depending on the industry, the economy, and a host of other factors. But, remember the point being made here. It is in the context of Time Management, which is little more than the timely completion of daily activities related to properly set goals. Your daily activities must be in keeping with long-term Personal Revenue Goals, quarterly or monthly objectives and your Domestic Financial Goals.

Think about it this way: an Elite manager of time should know how many new contacts (suspects) are needed each day to get enough appointments (prospects), to close enough sales (clients), to generate enough revenue, to reach the quarterly/monthly objectives necessary to meet his/her annual/long-term Personal Revenue Goal at work.

Your manager or sales supervisor may answer these questions for you. He or she may use a big bulletin board in the office so everyone can see what every seller in the company is doing (Las Vegas Engineering). The bottom line is…you must be able to answer this question at any time of any day in your "selling" life. If you cannot, then it's likely…YOU ARE WASTING SELLING TIME!

Here it is again:

How many contacts do you need in order to generate enough appointments, to close enough sales, to earn enough revenue, to reach the objectives necessary to meet your long-term goals?

Industry Variations

As always, in different industries or with different products, the information involved in developing revenue goals may differ. In real estate, you may need to add a column relating to "Listings Obtained." With insurance, you may need to get policy expiration dates in order to provide quotes or presentations 45 days or so prior to the expiration of the buyer's current policy. Like Listings in real estate, policy "x-dates" in insurance are the nuggets from which appointments, and thus sales, are made.

The point is not to let the terms or format become an excuse for skipping this step. If your company or sales manager isn't doing this for you, then you must do it for yourself. Once you've got pre-

Individual Self Management

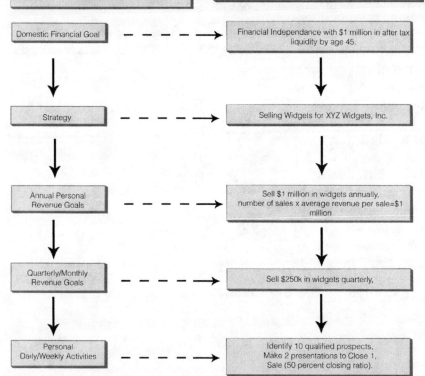

Domestic Mission
To become known in my community as a kind, fair, hardworking, productive member of society and to become a sincere, loving, kind parent and spouse, who displays compassion and understanding to family members, close friends, and neighbors. To conduct all relationships by displaying the qualities of understanding, patience, and tolerance in order to be liked, respected, and admired by the people I meet and know and who know me.

Professional Mission
To become known as the consummate professional seller in my field. To be knowledgeable about my products and services so that I can provide all buyers with a high quality affordable solution to their problems and needs. To be known as a person of the highest ethical standards, who will always be prepared, dependable, punctual, compassionate, and understanding. To be trusted, well liked, and admired by every client and prospect of my company.

Domestic Financial Goal → Financial Independance with $1 million in after tax liquidity by age 45.

Strategy → Selling Widgets for XYZ Widgets, Inc.

Annual Personal Revenue Goals → Sell $1 million in widgets annually, number of sales x average revenue per sale=$1 million

Quarterly/Monthly Revenue Goals → Sell $250k in widgets quarterly,

Personal Daily/Weekly Activities → Identify 10 qualified prospects, Make 2 presentations to Close 1, Sale (50 percent closing ratio).

vious year figures (either from your own experience or based on average production of other sellers in your company), you can put together meaningful production goals for the coming year. The appendix contains a sample worksheet for reducing an annual goal to daily activities in terms of prospects, x-dates, contacts, and so forth. But, it's just an example.

Depending on the product you sell or your market niche, prospecting activities, like gathering x-dates, can be done by phone, using the Internet, and/or by someone other than the seller. This leaves a greater part of each day for performing the more goal sensitive tasks of making presentations or sales calls.

Therefore, prospecting calls are among the most important things you can do each day, or that someone can do for you. Without these calls you won't make contact and without contacts you won't have prospects and, thus, you'll be left the opportunity to make sales only by cold calling. Goals, prospects, and daily activities are indelibly tied to one another.

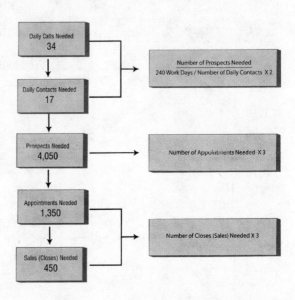

Goals, Prospects & Activities

Assumptions: a 33% closing ratio; a 33% conversion rate of contacts to prospects; a 33% conversion ratio of prospects to appointments; and, a 50% call ratio of calls that yield a contact.

Daily Calls Needed
34

Daily Contacts Needed
17

Number of Prospects Needed
240 Work Days / Number of Daily Contacts X 2

Prospects Needed
4,050

Number of Appointments Needed X 3

Appointments Needed
1,350

Number of Closes (Sales) Needed X 3

Sales (Closes) Needed
450

Chapter 20

REACHING YOUR GOALS

The secret to success is not about what you do. It's about who you are.—Lisa Harrington

Once you've established effective goals that meet the eight requirements itemized in the previous segment, you will ultimately be confronted with the micro level challenge of Time Management, the challenge of regulating daily activities so that goal-related tasks are performed—easier said than done.

Whether you are self-employed or work for a business, your daily routine is peppered with seemingly mandatory tasks that are not directly related to the achievement of goals or objectives—things like personnel issues, government reports, sales reports, spam, junk mail, interruptions, errands, phone calls, distractions, on and on. In fact, according to a time logging experiment I conducted (and will discuss in more detail later) and based only on number of tasks (vs. the length of the task), such activities—the "rabbits" of Time Management—can consume the majority of any poorly managed work day. That's why vigilance, habit, and repetition are the kingpins of effective Self and Time Management. Not wasting time on inappropriate, non-goal-related activities is not something you do once and then forget about. It is a constant daily, and often hourly, routine that you must develop the habit of performing.

For an Elite few, it may come naturally. Others have to work at it a little bit. And, unfortunately, there are always those who are simply incapable of managing their time efficiently or at all. Nonetheless, there are rules and basics that apply, which, if applied, can multiply your success and, thus, your on-the-job satisfaction a thousand-fold. I commend these concepts to you and ask that you implement them for one week. Don't look for excuses as to why they don't apply to you or your company or situation. Look for ways to improvise or adapt them to your unique environment. I believe that doing so for one week can only put you well on the road to having the habit of performing them for the rest of your working life.

Impediments and Costs
The first step to getting your goal-related activities done each day is to know what impedes you from getting them done. Secondarily, an important step in motivating you to take a new approach is to better understand the true cost of such impediments. Before looking at the four general proficiencies needed for better time management, we'll look at these two important areas: time management impediments and their true cost.

Time Logging
I found that my sales team already knew (or suspected) where they were wasting time, but objectively determining this and categorizing your prime time-wasters is still an extremely helpful exercise. Recalling my earlier story about Disney and Mike Vance, at one point during a sales retreat I asked all the sellers of my company to complete a time log for each day of one work week. I called every evening to remind them to begin in the morning and to fax it to me the following evening. I also asked them to account for any "unaccounted for" fifteen-minute periods. While the grumblings were quite pronounced, all agreed the results were revealing.

In fact, I suggest that you take, as a minimum, one work day to record your time—one day invested in the future, how can it hurt?

You can use the following chart to merely record every fifteen-minute segment of your time. In today's world this can be done electronically through e-mail, PDAs, or other such approaches. Either way, be honest and be complete. I promise you'll find it extremely instructive, especially if your co-workers do the same thing and a supervisor or manager categorizes and totals the responses, developing averages which can be discussed in a group setting. Often, the mere act of time logging makes a company and the individuals in it more productive, at least temporarily.

Daily Time Log

Name _____ Day _____ Date _____

Time	Activity	Priority	Interruptions
7:00 a.m.			
7:15			
7:30			
7:45			
8:00			
8:15			
8:30			
8:45			
9:00			
9:15			
9:30			
9:45			
10:00			
10:15			
10:30			
10:45			
11:00			
11:15			
11:30			
11:45			
12:00 p.m.			
12:15			
12:30			
12:45			
1:00			
2:15			
2:30			
2:45			
3:00			
3:15			
3:30			
3:45			
4:00			
4:15			
4:30			
4:45			
5:00			

Daily Carry-Overs

It is from a collection of over one hundred personal time logs identical to the one above—seventy-five from regional sellers, five of my own and others from a number of support staff—that I formulated the major "daily" impediments and barriers to achieving properly established "sales" goals.

Spending days analyzing, categorizing, and averaging how these disparate individuals spent their selling time, I was able to isolate what gets in the way of sellers meeting their established goals and objectives. Keep in mind, we're talking about impediments to achieving effective sales goals and objectives. From the time logs it was easy to see that some of my sellers had large daily carry-overs that grew and grew over time. That is, the tasks they needed to perform that were related to their goals, were not done and thus were "carried over" to the next day and the next day, until they were simply to overwhelming to perform. These talented sellers were consistently unable to meet their goals, even their shorter term objectives, and the reasons why were painfully obvious from their time logs and verified by their huge daily carry-overs and missed quotas.

Remember, their goals and objectives were, just like the rest of the sellers in the company, reasonable and achievable, time bound, written, communicated to others and consistent with all eight criteria of the "perfect" goal. Plus, these were qualified sellers who were both naturally talented and experienced using the face-to-face techniques covered in Platform I of this book. Yet they, unlike the rest, weren't meeting their goals. "Why not?" was the operative question. What was different about the activities and the self management of those who were failing?

Four Areas Of Time Management Proficiency

At our next sales meeting, I distributed everyone's time logs. First I removed the names and blacked out anything that would identify the person who had completed it so as not to embarrass anyone. Then, as a group, we reviewed the time logs and began consolidating the most prevalent time wasters of the company. In doing so, we came up with four general categories. Those categories assisted in the development and the gathering of tools, suggestions, hints, and other ideas helpful to becoming proficient at managing the time wasting activities (or non-activities) within each category. The four areas of basic time management proficiency are:

1.) Developing and managing a goal-related daily to-do list.

2.) Managing interruptions and time wasters so they don't unnecessarily impede completion of goal-related activities.

3.) Managing workspace, paperwork, e-mail, and faxes so that they don't unnecessarily impede completion of goal-related activities.

4.) Eliminating Procrastination.

What It Costs
As we move ahead through the following areas of proficiency, you'll find there are suggestions, steps, or other recommendations of things to do, to avoid, to amend or enhance that will assist you in meeting the particular proficiency being discussed. These steps or recommendations have value, immense value to you in terms of saving time—how much time and the value of the time saved will vary from individual to individual. However, it is a helpful exercise to think of each time saving activity in terms of "What It Costs" and secondarily how much money is saved or made as a result.

Let's say you have as a goal next year to net $192,000 in new sales commissions for yourself. That means, assuming 240 work days, you must net $16,000 each month, or $4,000 each week, on average, or…about $800 per day. If you are willing to work, say…a 10 hour day, every weekday, the value of your time is, roughly, $80 an hour. If you can save five hours a week, that's $1,600 saved or earned every month, assuming you wisely invest the saved time.

If you choose to work eight hours instead of 10, you have reduced your working time by 20 percent and thus increased the value of the time saved by 20 percent; $80 of value for each hour becomes $96 ($1.20 \times 80 = 96$). Either way, saving five hours a month is a matter of eliminating roughly fifteen to twenty wasted minutes from each day. Can you find 15 minutes in your time log? Most people can find much, much more.

Keep this formula in mind. Adapt it to Personal Revenue Goals and break it down to apply a value to a single hour of work, your work. In this way, you'll motivate yourself to better self management by understanding the true dollar cost of each wasted moment in each day of work.

Developing and Managing a Goal-Related Daily To-Do List

For those I've interviewed and according to every survey I've seen, including one of CEOs for Fortune 500 companies, daily routines were always managed by the same effective tool. Almost without exception, a daily to-do list was the most common of denominators. In one form or another—hard copy, maintained by an assistant or a secretary, electronically maybe even augmented with a PDA (Personal Digital Assistant)—the most successful sellers, CEOs, entertainers, sports figures…all utilize a daily to-do list to manage their daily activities.

In fact, according to the time log experiment above, every seller in my company utilized a to-do list. The only question was whether or not doing so helped them achieve their sales quotas, goals, and objectives. I found some were better at managing their time so as to get the "right" tasks done first. Others were not so enabled. As a team, we analyzed why such differences existed and found that there is more to a successful to-do list than just jotting down a few notes while you're standing in the kitchen each morning. Here are some guidelines for an effective to-do list.

Goal-Related To-Do List

A to-do list is little more than a personal efficiency tool. Its purpose is usually just to help you remember what to do and to save time moving from one task to the next. However, as my sales team soon began to learn, if structured properly, a to-do list can and should be much more. It can motivate. It can avoid or minimize Procrastination. And…it can ensure that the right tasks get done first and the wrong ones are done last or avoided altogether. How much time could this save you and how much is it worth?

At the end of each day, jot down the tasks that must be done the following day; include any carry-overs. Once you list the items that must be done the following day, prioritize them using A, B, and C, according to the following:

A—Those items that are to be done next and which directly relate to the achievement of your long-term goals or objectives. These should include any carry-over items not completed the previous day that were also labeled as an A. This should usually include activities that were part of the charts used in developing your goals or objectives, such as prospecting, x-dating, setting appointments, designing proposals, making presentations, etc.

B—Items that are not "directly" goal-related, but may be indirectly related to achieving goals because they enable you to achieve them or to complete goal-related activities. These could include requisitioning office supplies necessary to put together a proposal, calling the production department, or talking with IT about a PowerPoint presentation and so forth.

C—This includes non-goal-related items that must be completed as part of your job, but which do not directly or indirectly contribute to the achievement of your goals or objectives. Filling out expense reports might be one example. You should ask yourself what would happen if you didn't do a "C" item on your to-do list. If the answer is "nothing," then...don't do it! Typically, these items involve an in box or e-mails full of trade publications, spam, or correspondence that isn't related to your goals. It may be dealing with interesting, but non-goal-related office politics or employee problems, interruptions, or distractions. Bottom line, you are a seller. If it isn't related to meeting sales goals and nothing bad happens if you don't do it...don't do it! It's that simple.

It is often helpful to prioritize your to-do list within each category particularly A and B items by indicating the order of each item as an A1, A2, or an A3, B3, etc. This enables you to merely ask yourself…"What is the best use of my time, right now?" The answer will always be the next numbered item on your to-do list.

Managing Interruptions and Time Wasters So They Don't Unnecessarily Impede Your Goal-Related Activities
First things first. The time logs revealed one thing quite clearly; that the biggest wasters of time were the people who complained most about how other people wasted their time. In other words, someone else was always to blame.

My friend Bert was the perfect example. He wasn't even involved in my business unit (sales), but our offices were in close proximity and we had developed a kinship over the years. Eventually, we considered it part of our Monday morning routine to spend time telling each other how our golf game was developing—my slice, his hook. Those of you who play the game, understand that golfers can remember every detail of every shot, every club used, every putt, and the physical layout surrounding every shot they have ever made in every round of golf they've ever played. Amazing! Bert couldn't remember his appointments or to hand in his expense report, but he and I could easily remember the details of all 125 swings required to move a little white ball close to five miles, dropping it into 18 small holes along the way. I miss old Bert!

Eventually, we became morning water cooler buddies, spending the most important first hour of each day sipping coffee, recounting golf stories, sharing our home life and office gossip like we had nothing better to do. We occasionally even wasted each others time complaining about how others in the office were always wasting our time. It was only about 15 minutes each morning and didn't seem like much time was being wasted. Eventually, however, I was promoted to vice president of Marketing at our newest subsidiary and the luxury of those fifteen minutes began getting in the way of achieving my personal goals.

Despite my promotion and new responsibilities, Bert thought we should still keep our old relationship. He even complained to me that I thought I was too good to chat with him each morning like I used to. I felt bad and didn't want to lose Bert as a friend. At the same time, I had more work to do now with deadlines and pressure, and Bert would be a real friend if he didn't add to that pressure and let me get back to the tasks at hand—which he eventually did.

My question to you is..."How many Bert's do you know in your office?"

Interruption Contracts
The time logs told me that everyone has a Bert or two, perhaps more. And, they taught me that the very biggest waster of your time is you and the contracts you have with other people that give them the right to "interrupt" or waste your time. I blamed Bert when I should have been blaming myself.

From the time logs, we found that anything that interrupts a goal-oriented A1 task usually averages about 15 minutes—in fact, that's why the time logs were amended to reflect fifteen minute increments. By the time you get through with the interruption (e-mail, conversation, or phone call), go get another cup of coffee, relocate your stopping point, and get back up to speed, you've wasted 15 minutes (on average) even with the shortest interruption that may have only taken a few minutes.

Of course, some people have contracts with you that give them the right to interrupt—your boss, for example, or a customer with a problem, perhaps. I call this type of interruption contract an Express Interruption Contract. That is, it is expressly agreed in the employment arrangement that this person can interrupt you anytime he/she wishes to. Often it's something we have to deal with, although most bosses can detect when you are busy and may wish to leave you to your productive, goal oriented work.

Implied Interruption Contracts are those where my actions have implied to someone else that they have the right to interrupt me when the working relationship otherwise dictates that they do not. I had implied to Bert that it was okay to interrupt me anytime, especially in the mornings and especially Monday mornings. Breaking my contract with Bert was difficult, but it saved me almost five hours every month. By eliminating my other implied contracts, I discovered I had a full extra day in every week that no one else had (or maybe they were already utilizing it and I was not). And, I met my goals, was able to increase them in the future, and worked under less stress as deadlines no longer loomed quite so ominously. What a godsend it was when I finally began terminating my Implied Interruption Contracts.

To further manage interruptions and time wasters and to help you squeeze every available productive minute from your work day, you may consider the following helpful hints:

- Avoid interruptions from visitors who drop in. Greet them in the reception area. Ask your assistant to come get you in a specified amount of time.
- Stop being constantly available by cell phone. Consider turning it off, completely off, especially while you're working on a special project.
- Stop socializing during times set aside for projects.
- Cut down on the number of voluntary tasks you agree to.
- Schedule activities so you don't have too much or too little time for them.
- Prepare for the possibility of being kept waiting.
- Create an agenda for every meeting. Start meetings with "Okay, what do we need to accomplish during this meeting and how can we get there efficiently?" Or, "Does everyone have a copy of the agenda?"
- When working on something important, an A1 that requires concentration, keep your door closed, your phone on do not disturb, and your e-mail set to "not available."
- When someone interrupts you, ask "Can I talk with you about this later when I get to a good stopping point?" or "I'm right in the middle of something; can I buzz you in a few minutes?" In most cases, the hint will be taken and the time wasting conversation will never occur.

- Practice making mental notes of every time you avoid an interruption. Add them all up and assign fifteen minutes to each one, and divide by sixty (60). Calculate the dollar amount of the time you saved each week or month by multiplying by the dollar figure you assigned to each hour of your work day. I bet it's worth it!

Managing Workspace, Paperwork, E-mail, and Faxes So That They Don't Unnecessarily Impede Completion of Goal-Related Activities.

Work space management problems generally fall into one or all of three categories:

- *Poor space planning*—constantly getting up and down for items needed to complete important tasks.
- *Poor work habits*—each day a few more papers become permanent residents of your desk or new e-mails become permanent distractions in Outlook. You look at them or make decisions about them more than once, sometimes many times over long periods of time until, eventually, you do what should have been done in the first place; you toss or delete them.
- *Indecision*—you simply don't know what to do with the piles of paper on your desk, credenza, and bookshelf, or the e-mails, folders, and files on your computer.

When it comes to desk organization, stacks of paper are the single biggest problem. You don't have time to finish a project, so you leave it until morning. You're expecting an answer from XYZ Company by the end of the week, so you'll leave the file out until then. You didn't finish reading your e-mail, so you'll leave it until Monday. The only problem is that by the time Monday comes, there's more, much more.

Here are some ways to get your desk, paperwork, and immediate work environment under control.

- From a Las Vegas Engineering standpoint, a wider desk is better than a deeper one. Deep desks lend themselves to creating and maintaining stacks of paper, making it too easy for things to pile up and get lost. Go to an office supply store. Sit at different desks and in different chairs; when you find a combination that's materially better than what you have currently…buy it!

- Put your in box behind you, not in front of you where it acts as a distraction. Also, use three separate smaller boxes categorized as A, B, and C. Train your assistant on what items go in which box. Use a different color paper (yellow or buff) in your fax machine so faxes stand out in each in box.

- Handle each piece of paper and each e-mail only once. If possible, process each as it comes in, handle it the first time, and get it off your desk. If you can't handle it, make a decision… do something! Take some action even if it is just to route it to a co-worker for an opinion. Never organize by stacking paper or e-mails to get to later.

- Make it a rule to *always* re-file things. You can establish a special place (such as a desktop standing file) for current projects, but otherwise put everything away and out of site.

- Put loose papers in clearly labeled files ("To Do," "To Read," etc.) or color-coded ones (purple = medical, green = legal matters). Create similar folders for e-mails.

- Instead of asking yourself, "Could I possibly use this one day?" ask, "What's the worst thing that could happen if I throw this out?" If the answer is nothing, then toss it.

- Make a game out of seeing how much junk mail you can toss before you reach a certain spot. At home, try to pull out as much junk as you can before you reach your door or before reaching a designated spot such as the trash can in the garage.

- Instead of jotting down notes on scraps of paper and never knowing where to find them, establish an idea file in either hard copy or electronically. Buy a medium-sized, loose-leaf notebook with paper and dividers so you'll have one place to look when you want to refer back to that million-dollar idea.

- To keep track of deadlines, use a computer calendar, preferably one linked to your PDA. It is truly one of the most powerful time management tools available. Be sure to note a project's deadline on a date earlier than when it is due so you will be sure to finish it in time; use the built in "snooze" function in Outlook or similar desktop manager and coordinate it with your assistant's computer.

- Set aside time daily for doing paperwork (or e-mails). Choose an hour when there are few distractions—if at home, in the early morning before the family gets up; if at work, before the staff comes in. During this time, use an answering machine or your voice-mail system to screen calls or have your assistant hold calls, or have a coworker answer your phone.
- Clean up your desk every night to eliminate confusion when you begin the next morning. Before leaving, place tomorrow's to-do list prominently in the middle of your desk.
- Mind your Ds and Cs. Eliminate C items from your to-do list by using the four Ds, as follows:

  - Drop every task that doesn't truly need to be done;
  - Delegate everything someone else can do;
  - Delay tasks that are better left for another time; then
  - Do only those tasks that absolutely must be done.

- Tear up or crumple the letters, pamphlets, and miscellaneous hard copy you throw out so that you won't be tempted to retrieve any of it. Should you ever throw away something you later need (a rare occurrence in my experience), chances are you'll be able to get another copy. Besides, occasionally wishing you hadn't thrown something out is a small price to pay for being organized enough to quickly find the items you kept.

E-Mail
Recently, I was cleaning out a closet at my home and came across a picture that had been taken of me at my office. It was 1995 and I was sitting at my desk. Behind me were my three in boxes clearly labeled as A, B and C. The C box was filled mostly with trade magazines and junk mail that I now tell my assistant to toss. The B box and the A box contained mostly letters from clients, customers, or other important communications that I would likely have to respond to in some fashion. It's likely that the letters that stuffed my in boxes represented those I had received in just one or two days.

Contrast that with today's environment when, for the last twelve months, I have received only two letters total. Last year, I received only one and it came from an elderly gentleman who is the only one in his office that still doesn't use e-mail. From roughly 500 letters a year to only two a year. Today, virtually every piece of correspondence arrives electronically, unless it was from the government or had to be sent certified. Chances are it's the same in your office.

It's hard to find anyone who isn't using electronic mail. It is, after all, an easy, fast way to correspond and represents immense time-saving efficiency. Unfortunately, because it's so easy to use, many are just chatting when they should be working and the quantity of junk e-mail is growing exponentially.

You've got to guard against letting this powerful productive tool eat up the time you could otherwise spend on goal-related activities. Here are some ideas you may find helpful:

- Checking e-mail every few minutes is a huge time-waster. Turn off the "incoming message" alarm that dings on some programs and establish certain times each day when you check e-mail—perhaps first thing in the morning, before lunch, after lunch, and at the end of the day. This schedule permits you to catch any urgent messages before they are "old" and yet you don't fracture your concentration by checking e-mail all day.
- Use the "preview" function to scan through your e-mail, deleting unwanted messages (spam, jokes, mail order advertisements) without opening them.
- Become proficient at creating and managing electronic folders so that you can save important e-mails by topic or sender. If a client calls and wants to know when he sent information to you, you can open the client folder in your e-mail program and quickly locate the information you need.
- Consider forwarding e-mails you want to read, but aren't necessary to be read during work or they aren't directly goal-related, to your home computer and reading them later or read them from your laptop when you're on the road or waiting in a doctor's office.

- If you get a great deal of e-mail and cannot possibly process it all each day, answer the more important items immediately, then create a "To Answer" folder where you put any messages that you want to answer at a later date. You may be able to color code incoming e-mail. Your boss's messages should arrive in red; those from staff members might be green; any e-mail where you're simply on a copied list could be blue. Some people save their To Answer e-mails for a trip, spending time on the plane clearing out messages.
- Keep your own messages clear and to the point.
- Always use the Subject Line and state clearly what the e-mail is about.
- On more than one occasion an overly casual e-mail message has been interpreted as being an insult to the receiver. If you're writing to people other than family or close co-workers, set your e-mail up as a regular business letter. It should begin with "Dear" and conclude with "Sincerely," or however you usually conclude a business letter.
- Keep paragraphs short—one- to two-sentence paragraphs are easiest for the recipient to scan.
- Only copy those people who really need to receive your message.
- Both at home and at work, think before you press "Send." You'll be glad you did.
- Use e-mail thoughtfully. Don't copy everyone in the office or everyone who was copied to you just because you can.
- Because e-mail is often so casual, an exchange can go on longer than it needs to. If the other person e-mails you "Thanks," you needn't e-mail back "You're welcome." Try to anticipate when you might encounter a continuous string of messages and conclude with "Thanks in advance" or "No reply needed."
- Setting your program for an auto-reply when you are out of the office can be helpful so that people know they are unlikely to hear back from you immediately. If you do set up auto reply, unsubscribe from any e-mail lists while you are away to prevent the auto-reply from bouncing you off those lists permanently.
- Because 70 percent of all e-mail is spam, use an e-mail filter. Check your software program or Internet Service Provider to

see if there is a way to filter out spam and send it to a bulk e-mail folder. Group incoming e-mails by putting spam into one category that can be easily deleted as a group.

Computer Calendars & PDAs

Calendar software, like that found in Outlook and PDAs usually features an appointment book, address book, To-Do lists, and a space for notes and more; it is one of the greatest efficiency tools ever invented, in my opinion.

- Rescheduling is virtually automatic. Your appointments, along with notes, instructions and details can be moved to any other day or time with just a few key strokes.
- They inform you of your availability at a glance. If you need to know if you have any free time next week, a click instantly provides you with the entire week's schedule.
- You have dual or group scheduling. Both managers and their assistants input the schedule from their own computers, making it easy to coordinate and stay up-to-date. Group scheduling and departmental meetings are also scheduled and updated with attendee responses and scheduling conflicts transmitted. (You choose how much of your calendar you want to make available for public scheduling. The rest can be kept private.)
- Any appointment can be set to automatically appear.
- Your daily carry-overs can be highlighted until all tasks are complete.

Formerly considered an executive toy, today's electronic organizers are used by a wide range of people. Early versions of PDAs required entering material directly into the device. Today's PDAs generally synchronize with an owner's computer, and calendar dates as well as phone numbers and addresses need be entered into only one place (either the computer or the handheld device) for the information to be reflected in both. In addition to functioning as a calendar and phone book, the new models of PDAs may also handle e-mail and word processing and run games—some even have spreadsheet capabilities. Consumers can also select a telephone/PDA combo unit. The reviews of these combo devices are surprisingly good.

Because most combo PDAs are larger and a bit bulkier than a cell phone, some people still prefer having two separate devices. I highly recommend that you either get one or begin investigating the cost and benefit of doing so.

Eliminating Procrastination
Unless there truly is a better time to do a task or something is needed before it can be done properly, it is never wise to delay that which has to be done.

Of course, everybody procrastinates sometimes, about some things. The most enabling comment of the chronic procrastinator is usually something like…"First, I need to get this out of the way." Usually, the stuff I did to keep from doing the stuff I should always sounded something like…"getting stuff out of the way." When I had an "overwhelming A" that needed to be done, but that couldn't be done easily or in just one day or a few days, I usually found I had to finally read the trade magazines that I hadn't read in a month or the junk mail that had gathered in my in box. Then, once I "cleared things off my desk" or "completed some pending items" (or whatever), I could begin.

Procrastination generally signals some type of internal conflict. While we've made the decision to do something, there is still something holding us back. The task is overwhelming, has too many details, is confusing, or we don't know exactly how to begin or what to do. Often, we'll find that we overestimate the time needed, or, the opposite, we think we have forever to finish something.

Maybe, we think if we wait long enough the task will go away, be cancelled, or postponed.

We often fear turning in a report or finishing a project because we worry about failing on "Judgment Day." We don't want to be blamed if it isn't good enough. After all, if we never complete the project, no one will hold us responsible for its quality.

We delay until the last minute and then, if it doesn't measure up, we say, "Oh, I would have done better if I'd had more time."

Fear of Success
If we complete something and succeed, will we be able to continue to live up to that standard? How will others relate to us once we are successful?

Failing to remember the times when emergencies came up during the allocated time of a project, people who feel they work best under pressure purposely delay to create that last minute adrenalin rush.

Procrastinators Anonymous
Frankly, the answers aren't easy for the chronic procrastinator who doesn't want to stop. Conversely, if you want to stop, most every answer is easy.

Here are some easy answers that work for me:

1.) **Make a Procrastination list and keep it handy.**
   - Is there a pattern to your procrastination; certain tasks, times or situations?
   - What bad things happen; anxiety, rushed work product, missed deadlines?
   - When you procrastinated for a long time and then finally did it, what finally got you going?

2.) **When you find yourself procrastinating, consider the following:**
   - What does the procrastination help you avoid?
   - Ask if you truly want to pay the price of delaying.
   - Always ask yourself, "What is the best use of my time right now?" If it's not what you're doing, stop doing it and do the right thing.
   - When you are procrastinating on paper work, use the Measles Approach: clip a red pen to the paper, form, or document; then, whenever you pick it up or look at it

without finishing it, put a red dot in the corner. Eventually, you'll have to get it done or your paper will look like it has the measles.

- Whenever you sense you may be putting something off, just say to yourself, DO IT NOW!
- Use the Swiss Cheese Approach. Often it is best to do only a small piece of an overwhelming project. Maybe just jotting down some steps would be helpful or just reviewing some ideas or an outline. Whatever it is, if it's related to an A1 task, it's got to be a better use of your time than doing something merely to put it off. The Swiss Cheese Approach works wonders in nibbling away at the big tasks, so eventually you get immersed in it enough that you're motivated to finish the job.

An Important Summary

In the beginning of this Platform I defined the nature of Self Management by describing the macro and micro levels as subsets. Specifically, I said:

> *At the micro level (the level of day-to-day activities), as long as your tasks relate to the achievement of properly set goals, effectiveness can be measured merely by the "timely" completion of those tasks over the time period specified in your goal. Properly setting sales goals, those that achieve your personal revenue goals, then making sure that daily activities relate to those goals is the macro level — the sum total of the two is self management.*

But…there is slightly more to Self Management than setting goals and completing daily activities related to those goals. There is something a bit more impalpable, something I believe is related to an innate sense of punctuality.

Former Chief Justice of the US Supreme Court Oliver Wendell Holmes, Jr., said, "There are two types of people in this world, those who say there are two types of people in this world, and everybody else." I fall into the former category. I believe there are two types of people in this world. While they could be described in many different ways depending on which characteristic you decide to focus, in the context of this book, and particularly within the context of Platform III, I look at people as being those who are either "on time" or those who are "late."

Some people, no matter what the occasion, no matter how important or how prepared they may be, simply cannot or will not arrive on time, for anything. In the company of others or at the urging of friends or family members, they can occasionally be on time. But, left to their own devices, they will not arrive for anything at the prescribed hour.

I recall a job interviewing process myself and several of my co-workers went through. We were trying to hire an assistant to help in-house staff that had become so overworked their lack of ability to get their jobs done was beginning to affect our ability to meet sales goals. The person we would hire would be another staff assistant for all the sellers in the company. This person would help by answering phones and manning a help desk for both hardware and software problems from existing customers and by helping the company's fifteen sellers prospect, make appointments, and more. In other words, he/she would have to multi-task, be organized, and punctual in all matters.

To minimize our time away from goal-related tasks, we had scheduled a number of interviews with various applicants, back-to-back, all in the same day. We allowed for one hour interviews with 15 minutes in between. Things went fine until the most qualified applicant showed up 20 minutes late. She came into the interview and apologized profusely. "No problem" we all said, "it happens." And, indeed, it wasn't a problem. After all, we had padded the interviews with extra time and allowed for 15 minutes between each one. And frankly, the others didn't look as good on paper as this one did and we were so eager to hire someone we could easily overlook the 20 minutes of our time that she had already wasted.

That is until she blamed her tardiness on traffic!

An automobile accident would've been an acceptable excuse or even just car trouble, a flat tire maybe. But…by blaming traffic she was telling us she had left for a cross-town appointment too late; best case, she miscalculated the time it would take to drive to our office or to find it. The real reason for being tardy was non-lunch hour, non-rush hour…traffic. And the most telling reason to never hire this person was that she seemed to think it was an acceptable excuse for being 20 minutes late for a "JOB INTERVIEW!"

Sorry…not at my company, not working for me, not when the sales and careers of others are at stake!

The Morning Hour(s)
In my seminars on Time Management, I would often start by telling my audience that medical science has been able to determine what time of day human beings are at their sexual peaks. That is, what time of day are they most amorous and most likely (and able) to engage in sexual relations with their spouses or significant others? It always got their attention.

Answers varied based on many factors. Often, females would say it was in the evening, "when the stars are out" or "when the moon is shining"…the so-called romantic hours. Men would sometimes, jokingly, say they were ready anytime. Eventually, after my students got through chuckling and joking, they turned to me for an answer…I tried not to disappoint.

The fact is that science has determined that both men and women are at their sexual peaks in the early morning, usually right after they wake up from a good night's sleep. Research, measuring blood pressure, hormone levels, energy, alertness, indeed…our "senses," proves we are at our peeks when we have just concluded an evening of comfortable, restful sleep. We awake, slowly, but arrive at a point where we are refreshed, eager, and alert—the most alert we will be all day long. In the mornings, at work, we are at our most creative and are most able to maintain focus or complete difficult tasks. From the morning's high, it's all downhill until we crash again that evening.

I mention this because one morning hour has essentially the same value as two afternoon hours in terms of benefit, creativity, and focus. Therefore, it isn't just me talking about the value of starting early—to the contrary, it is an important Time Management principle based on scientific fact; those who regularly start early can get more done in less time. Surveys show that 70 percent of all sales are closed before lunch.

Rethink how you spend your early morning hours at work. Are you wasting time at the water cooler? Are you chatting too long at the coffee machine? Are you just arriving while others are already working? Or...are you utilizing the most productive minutes of the day actually doing those A1 tasks your to-do list says need to be done?

I'm reminded of a saying I hear quite often from a friend and co-worker who is also a talented meeting planner named Cindy. The meetings she runs often have thousands of attendees and feature world-renown speakers and entertainers. And, because they last for several days, the entire conference, and every event at the conference, must start on time or the schedule is permanently delayed. At her preconference meetings, Cindy therefore reminds everyone that, "To be early is to be on time; to be on time is to be late; and, to be late is unacceptable!"

Our time logs were quite revealing in this regard. Some sellers always got a late start and were behind the rest of the day. Our North Carolina representative would inevitably begin attacking his goal-related activities around 10:00 a.m. when others were already on their way to their second appointment of the day. There were others on the team who also seemed to waste the first hour of every day and the reason was painfully consistent. They spent much of that time reviewing what tasks were left over from the previous day and what needed to be put on the to-do list they were currently assembling. Some were also just naturally slow starters in the morning.

But our time logging revealed these deficiencies and as a group we could see the benefit of "starting early" on a daily basis and on those overwhelming tasks we were sometimes confronted with. Like the previously mentioned Swiss Cheese Approach, starting early is the best way to fight procrastinating on important or over-whelming tasks. When you know you have something you must do, get started on it right away. A head start can be habit forming. It is its own reward and it motivates you to keep going and before you know it, well...before you know it, the job is done.

Finally, Elite Status rarely flows to those lacking a sense of urgency, especially with regard to goal-related activities. Be punctual in all matters. Leave early for appointments; yes, even "hurry up and wait" is better than keeping a buyer or true friend waiting, especially if you are the one who chose the time and are trying to gain something with your use of someone else's time. No excuses, no exceptions, no traffic to blame...start early, be on time!

EPILOGUE

Once a person says, "This is who I really am, what I am all about, what I was really meant to do," it is easier to decide how to spend one's time...David Viscott

As the head of a voluntary, non-profit association, my father often used a phrase to describe the requisite qualities of someone aspiring to serve on its board of directors.

"To be on this board," he would say, "you need only demonstrate you have the time, the talent, and the inclination to serve others."

My father's credo was simple enough to apply to virtually every endeavor of any worth or weight, not just voluntary board service. I believe anyone could benefit by rethinking those three simple words—time, talent, and inclination.

Time—Live Your Last Lecture
I referenced earlier the importance of time perspective and how success is largely contingent on how one perceives time, as either short-term or long-term. But, there's more to it than just how high you aim when driving—right in front of the car or down the road. There's also the question of whether you're even on the right road, or driving the right car.

A helpful exercise is to decide what lessons you would impart to others if they were the last lessons you could ever give. Think of the points you would include in what might be your last lecture; the one you would give if your time was running out.

Randy Pausch, who has lectured on time management and wrote or co-authored five books and over 70 articles, was a successful and talented computer science professor at Carnegie Mellon University (CMU) and was asked to do just that—to participate in a lecture series in which respected professors gave presentations as though it were the last lecture they could ever give.

Unlike the others, Randy Pausch didn't have to pretend. While preparing his "last lecture," doctors discovered he had pancreatic cancer and only three to six months to live. That's three to six months to fight for life, to protect the future of a wife and three children, and to both embrace and come to grips with his own mortality—a list most cannot complete in a lifetime.

Randy's last lecture was one of the most provocative and inspiring talks in CMU's history. And, one of the best attended. It became a book titled, *The Last Lecture*, and generated hundreds of thousands of Internet hits. The popularity of Randy's talk was due in large measure to the realization that a time management expert, running out of time, would surely understand its' true value and thus have valuable insights for others.

I would now ask you…if you had only three months to live and had to tell others how they should be spending their time, what would you tell them to do?

Once you have the answer…follow your own advice!

Talent—Even Talented People Need Feedback
I found my most talented sellers were the most difficult to convince of the value of the skills in this book.

Naturally talented people sometimes think they don't need sales training or that managing time is, in itself, a waste of time. They often see peer feedback and constructive criticism only as necessary evils—not potential career enhancers.

When you think of improving your level of talent, I suggest you do three things. First, look to where you can make the most improvement, not where improving is the easiest or would be the most fun. Second, confront and eliminate any fear you may have of failure or rejection. And finally, emulate success by looking to those who are successful for inspiration and training.

Inclination—Climbing The "Brick Walls"
We can't all become doctors, lawyers, or college professors, but most of us have what it takes to reach the top of any profession or trade. We have the time and the talent, but may lack sufficient motivation, that is... the "inclination" to do what's necessary.

Billionaire H. L. Hunt said that success is really just a matter of deciding what you want and what you are willing to give up, specifically...

> *Decide what you want, decide what you are willing to exchange for it. Establish your priorities and go to work.*

In striving for our goals, we all meet difficult tasks, the "brick walls" that appear insurmountable and make us question the true value of the goal or the direction in which we are headed. But, brick walls are really...

> *...to stop the people who don't want it bad enough...they are there so we can show how badly we want something.*

In other words, barriers to success merely delineate between those who wanted something and those who only thought they wanted something.

Having read this book, having practiced and taken to heart its many lessons, points, and examples, you have the skills to become an Elite Seller in today's world economy. The question now is, what are you willing to give up in order to get what you want?

Are you willing to work a little harder, a little smarter? Are you willing to study a little longer, scrimp, and save a little more than others?

Are you willing to climb over a few brick walls?

If so, you have not only ascended the three Platforms of Success, you now have the necessary "Time, Talent, and Inclination" to succeed.

I wish you the best of luck on the rest of your journey!

ACKNOWLEDGEMENTS AND SOURCES

I have to start by recognizing Xerox Learning Systems (XLS) as the source for the foundation of the selling skills provided in Platform I. It was from XLS's cassette tape learning programs that I learned teaching selling is largely a matter of teaching someone how to develop new habits. If it were not for the "scientific" approach XLS used to categorize selling skills and teach the novice how to apply them, I would never have been able to put this book together. As well, the concept of "charting" conversations or sales calls came to me from XLS and provided the mental template for the summary flow charts used to illustrate some of the skills in Platform I.

The Caliper Corporation, Herb Greenberg, and Patrick Sweeney, and their many presentations on hiring the right sales person, should also be mentioned. They were the source for several concepts used in this book and in the classes I used to teach many years ago. This is particularly true for the sections explaining how Ego Drive, Empathy, and Intelligence interrelate to form a successful seller's personality. If you liked this book, I would definitely recommend that you read the New York Times best seller, *Succeed on Your Own Terms*, coauthored by Greenberg and Sweeney.

Likewise, I'd like to thank Dr. John Lee (Time, Life & Lee) who provided me with much of the framework for the time management principles in the final unit. His stories and anecdotes, his lessons and leadership, were not only informative but quite inspirational in the early years of my career.

I'd like to thank Lisa Harrington, whose advice and suggestions were most helpful and who was the first to read this book cover to cover. And Larry Thompson, CPA, who double-checked my math; thank goodness!

Next, to the thousands of students from my sales or time management classes and the sellers who worked for (and with) me, you have my undying gratitude. You may not have known, but I was learning more from you than you were from me. I also wish to thank the thousands who suffered through a sales call or a group presentation from me. Your patience and feedback brought the skills and their categorization to complete focus in writing this book.

Finally, I took my personal experiences, and those of my students and sales team, and developed skill sets in keeping with available scientific data on persuasion and the psychology of buying and selling. The major reference was the book below called, *Yes! 50 Scientifically Proven Ways to Be Persuasive*. Most of the verbal skills in Platform I were structured using studies highlighted in this book by Drs. Goldstein, Martin, and Cialdini. I also used *Advanced Selling Strategies* by Brian Tracy as a source for true life anecdotes, historical parallels, and a collection of some of the best inspirational stories you can find anywhere.

Finally, in addition to the references below, I would be remiss if I didn't state that a good bit of all three platforms came from net surfing. For example, I discovered the story on Randy Pausch while Googling under Time Management. Unfortunately, the night before I wrote these words I saw on the TV that Randy died yesterday (July 25, 2008) at the age of 47. His cancer, the chemo, the drugs, took their toll during his final days, but…not on his spirit. I urge you to learn of Randy Pausch's intriguing journey and heroic battle with death by reading his book titled, *The Last Lecture*. I promise you'll develop a whole new perspective on the value of time and how to invest in it.

Also, don't hesitate to read the books and sites below for inspiration and information. You may be able to expand on what I provided here, which I originally obtained from one or more of these hard copy sources or Internet locations.

SOURCES

Abrams, Rhonda with Julie Vallone. Winning Presentation in a Day. Palo Alto, CA: The Planning Shop, 2005.

Albom, Mitch. for one more day. New York: Hyperion, 2006.

Bayan, Richard. Words That Sell. New York: McGraw-Hill, 2006.

Beckwith, Harry. Selling the Invisible: A Field Guide to Modern Marketing. New York: Warner Books, 1997.

———. What Clients Love: A Field Guide for Growing Your Business. New York: Warner Books, 2003.

Bettger, Frank. How I Raised Myself from Failure to Success in Selling. New York: Simon & Schuster, 1982.

Brooks, William T. Perfect Phrases for the Sales Call. New York: McGraw-Hill, 2006.

Brown, Paul and Alison Davis. Your Attention, Please. Avon, MA: Adams Media, 2006.

Curtis, Drew. It's Not News, It's FARK: How Mass Media Tries to Pass off Crap as News. New York: Gotham Books, 2007.

Cialdini, R. B. Influence: Science and Practice, 4th ed. Boston: Allyn & Bacon, 2001

Debelak, Don. Perfect Phrases for Business Proposals & Business Plans. New York: McGraw-Hill, 2006.

Duncan, Todd. High Trust Selling. Nashville, TN: Thomas Nelson Publishers, 2002.

Ferriss, Timothy. 4-Hour Workweek, The. New York: Crown Publishers, 2007.

Freese, Thomas A. Secrets of Question Based Selling: How the Most Powerful Tool in Business Can Double Your Sales Results. Naperville, IL: Sourcebooks, Inc., 2000.

Girard, Joe with Robert L. Shook. How to Close Every Sale. New York: Warner Business Books, 1989.

Gleeson, Kerry. Personal Efficiency Program, The: How to Get Organized to Do More Work in Less Time, 3rd ed. Hoboken, NJ: John Wile & Sons, Inc., 2004.

Goldstein, Noah, Steve Martin, and Robert Cialdini. Yes! 50 Scientifically Proven Ways to Be Persuasive. New York, New York: Free Press, a division of Simon and Schuster, 2008.

Greenberg, Herb, Harold Weinstein, and Patrick Sweeney. How to Hire and Develop Your Next Top Performer. New York: McGraw-Hill, 2001.

——— and Patrick Sweeney. Succeed on Your Own Terms. New York: McGraw-Hill, 2006.

Gschwandtner, Gerhard. Sales Closing Book, The. New York: McGraw-Hill, 2007.

Hamper, Robert J. and L. Sue Baugh. Handbook for Writing Proposals. Chicago, IL: NTC Business Books, 1995.

Hansen, Patrick Henry. Winning Sales Presentations: Presentation Strategies for Modern-Day Sales People. Alpine, UT: Brave Publishing, Inc., 2006.

Harrington, Lisa. Six Steps to Success. Tallahassee, FL: FAIA, 2001.

Hindle, Tim. Making Presentations. New York: DK Publishing, Inc., 1998.

Jones, Frances Cole. How to Wow. New York: Ballantine Books, 2008.

Klein, Ruth. Everything Guide to Being a Sales Rep, The. Avon, MA: Adams Media, 2006.

Koegel, Timothy J. Execptional Presenter, The. Austin, TX: Greenleaf Book Group Press, 2007.

Maggio, Rosalie. Art of Talking to Anyone, The. New York: McGraw-Hill, 2005.

Mancini, Marc. Time Management. New York: McGraw-Hill, 2003.

Mayer, David G. and Herbert Greenberg. "What Makes a Good Salesman?" Harvard Business Review. Boston, MA: 1964.

Maxwell, John C. Your Road Map for Success. Nashville, TN: Thomas Nelson Publishers, 2002.

McClain, Gary. Presentations: Proven Techniques for Creating Presentations That Get Results, 2nd ed. Avon, MA: F+W Publications, Inc., 2007.

McCormick, Blaine. Ben Franklin, America's Original Entrepreneur. Entrepreneur Press, www.entrepreneurpress.com, 2005.

Organize Yourself! A Service to Get Your Life Organized. Experience Publishing, Inc., and John Wile & Sons, http://organizeyourselfonline.com/.

Patterson, Kerry, Joseph Grenny, Ron McMillan, and Al Switzler. Crucial Conversations: Tools for Talking When Stakes Are High. New York: McGraw-Hill, 2002.

Pausch, Randy with Jeffrey Zaslow. The Last Lecture, 1st ed. New York: Hyperion Press, 2007.

Perlman, Alan M. Perfect Phrases for Executive Presentations. New York: McGraw-Hill, 2006.

Poscente, Vince. Age of Speed, The. Austin, TX: Bard Press, 2008.

Rosen, Keith. Complete Idiot's Guide to Closing the Sale, The. New York: The Penguin Group, 2007.

Runion, Meryl. How to use Power Phrases. New York, NY: McGraw-Hill, 2004.

Rye, David E. 1,001 Ways to Inspire Your Organization, Your Team and Yourself. Franklin Lakes, NJ: Book-mart Press, 1998.

Schiffman, Stephan. Ask Questions, Get Sales: Close the Deal and Create Long-Term Relationships, 2nd ed. Avon, MA: Adams Media, 2005.

Tracy, Brian. Advanced Selling Strategies. New York, NY: Simon and Schuster, 1995.

Walther, George R. Heat Up Your Cold Calls. Chicago, IL: Dearborn Trade Publishing, 2005.

Ziglar, Zig with Krish Dhanam, Bryan Flanagan, and Jim Savage. Top Performance: How to Develop Excellence in Yourself and Others. Grand Rapids, MI: Fleming H. Revell, 2003.

APPENDIX

LEARNING SNAPSHOTS

PLATFORM I

- **Your Sales Personality**—Drive, Empathy, and Intelligence.

- **Drive**—The inner need to persuade others.

- **Empathy**—The capacity to recognize the clues and cues provided by others in order to relate effectively to them.

- **Intelligence**—The ability to apply knowledge you have and to quickly acquire knowledge you don't have.

- **The Elite Mix**—Responses to customer statements made by Elite Sellers have a "structure" that reflects the perfect mix of Empathy and Ego Drive.

- **A Product Feature**—A characteristic of your product or service usually expressed in a word or a phrase.

- **A Product Benefit**—The satisfaction of a buyer need provided by a feature of your product or service.

- **The Secret(s) of Elite Sellers**—1) Questioning to get buyers to talk; 2) Listening and responding appropriately when they do; and, 3) Closing the sale.

- **Getting Around the Bases**—1) *Question* to uncover buyer needs that your product or service can satisfy. 2) *Satisfy* uncovered needs with benefits of your proposal, product, or service. 3) Then, *Close* the sale by gaining the desired buyer commitment.

- **Question Statements**—A statement made by the seller, followed by a pause.

- **General Questions**—Those that encourage the buyer to speak freely about a topic of his or her choosing or that stimulates the buyer to expand on something already stated or agreed.

- **Specific Questions**—Those that steer the sales conversation to specific topics of your choosing and limits buyer responses (sometimes to short one or two-word answers), usually in topic areas you have chosen.

- **Specific Benefit Statement**—Made during the sales call when buyer expresses a need as a result of questions or a Question Statement followed by questions. 1) *Expand* on the buyer's need by repeating the need or problem using buyer's language to both expand and confirm its importance. 2) Then, *Introduce* the appropriate benefit or feature that solves or answers the need.

- **Initial Benefit Statement**—Made at the beginning of a sales call, without the buyer expressing a need. 1) Describe an assumed general need. 2) Answer the need with a general benefit of your product or service.

- **General Benefit Statement**—Made anytime during the sales call when questions aren't appropriate to steer the customer to a new topic. 1) Describe an assumed general need. 2) Answer that need with a general benefit of your product or service.

- **Closing Statement**—1) Summarize the benefits of your product or service agreed to during the call; and, 2) Request the appropriate commitment.

- **Acceptance**—The buyer is listening, providing information, and reacting favorably to what you say. Continue to ask general questions, followed by specific questions, and listen for opportunities to introduce a product benefit and close.

- **Skepticism**—The buyer does not believe something you've said. You need to offer proof.

- **Proof Statement**—1) Restate the benefit; 2) Offer proof; and 3) Draw the conclusion for the buyer.

- **Indifference**—The buyer has no need for the benefits of your product and provides no information about needs or problems. You must use either specific questions or General Benefit Statements to direct the buyer to areas of need.

- **Extreme Indifference**—The buyer isn't responding to any questions, general or specific, or to benefit statements with anything relevant. Offer a Closing statement followed by General then Specific questions if necessary.

- **Objection**—Is strong opposition to or disagreement with a feature, or lack of a feature, of your product or service.

- **Incorrect Assumptions (easy objections)**—Are those that incorrectly assumed something about your product. Usually based on incorrect information, rumors, or misinterpretations of something the buyer read, deduced, heard or...assumed. 1) Expand the objection by rephrasing it in question form; and 2) Handle it immediately, offering proof if necessary.

- **Perceived Drawbacks (difficult objections)**—Are those based on accurate information in the description of a product feature or lack of a desired feature or benefit. 1) Minimize the objection by rephrasing it in question form; and 2) Use specific questions to lead the customer to benefits (either old ones or new ones yet introduced) that offset the Perceived Drawback.

- **Basic Analogy**—A simple reference to something else, usually an animate object(s) or situation or example used, to describe your product or a feature of your product or to make a point to the buyer.

- **Interactive Analogy**—Used to capture buyers' imaginations and get them to participate in both the analogy and the selling conversation; usually the seller describes a simple problem, then asks the buyer for the obvious solution.

PLATFORM II

1.) Ethos—Character and Credibility
2.) Pathos—Emotion and Delivery
3.) Logos—Logic and Content

Ten Problems in Most Sales Presentations

1.) They are too long.
2.) They are too complicated.
3.) They sell only features.
4.) They are poorly structured.
5.) Materials have errors, both typographical and technical.
6.) Materials are amateurish or poorly designed.
7.) They don't offer proof for the important points.
8.) Audience management is lacking.
9.) The presenter has an uninspiring delivery.
10.) There is no commitment requested of the audience.

Steps to A Successful Presentation

Step #1—State the purpose of the presentation and make a list of the important points and sub-points you want to make.

Step #2—Develop an outline arranging your main points in a logical and appropriate sequence, placing sub-points, also in a logical and appropriate sequence, beneath them.

Step #3—Write out your introductory comments and your opening Initial Benefit Statement.

Step #4—Write out the General Benefit Statements you will use to introduce each point of your presentation and develop transitional language to move you from one point to the next.

Step #5—Write out your concluding comments, including a summary of what you've told the audience, and request a commitment or some action or follow up on their part.

Step #6—Rehearse your presentation using a stop watch. Refine it accordingly. Rehearse it again.

Step #7—Decide on graphics and put the first draft together using the graphics you will use.

Step #8—Using a stop watch, rehearse your presentation again, using the visuals and in front of a live audience of friends, co-workers, or family members. Focus on your manner, presentation style, and delivery.

Step #9—Revise based on any constructive criticism from #8.

PLATFORM III

To be effective, a properly set goal must meet all eight of the following characteristics. It must:

1.) Be Specific.
2.) Be Measurable.
3.) Be Attainable.
4.) Be Time Bound.
5.) Be Meaningful.
6.) Be Controllable.
7.) Be Written.
8.) Be Communicated to Others.

Four Areas of Time Management Proficiency

1.) Developing and managing a goal-related daily to-do list.
2.) Managing interruptions and time wasters so they don't unnecessarily impede completion of goal-related activities.
3.) Managing workspace, paperwork, e-mail, and faxes so that they don't unnecessarily impede completion of goal-related activities.
4.) Eliminating procrastination.

Illustration 1

Seller's Previous Year-End Results

1. Total Revenue Generated by Seller = _____
2. Total Number of Sales Closed by Seller = _____
3. Total Commissions Paid to Seller = _____
4. Total Number of Contacts by Seller—phone, = _____
   e-mail, etc.
5. Total Number of X-Dates, if Applicable = _____
6. Total Number of Proposals, Presentations, = _____
   or Sales Calls Made by Seller

Illustration 2

Seller's Annual Production Goals

A. New Commission* Goal = _____
B. Average Sale = _____ (1. divided by 2.)
C. Average Commission % = _____ (3. divided by 1.)
D. Average Commission per Sale = _____ (B x C)
E. Number of Sales Needed = _____ (A divided by D)
F. Number of Proposals Needed per Sale = _____ (6. divided by 2.)
G. Total Number of Proposals Needed = _____ (E x F)
H. Number of Ex-Dates Needed per Proposal = _____ (5. divided by 6.)
I. Total Number of Ex-Dates Needed = _____ (G x H)
J. Number of Contacts Needed per Ex-Date = _____ (4. divided by 5.)
K. Total Number of Contacts Needed = _____ (I x J)
L. Number of Contacts Needed per Sale = _____ (K divided by E)
M. Number of Ex-Dates Needed per Sale = _____ (I divided by E)

Illustration 3

Seller's Daily Activity Goals

Annual Selling Time Available: 200 Days (eliminating weekends, holidays, vacations)

Contacts Needed = _____ (K divided by 200)
Ex-Dates Needed = _____ (I divided by 200)
Proposals Needed = _____ (G divided by 200)

Courtesy of Elite Selling, The Florida Association of Insurance Agents.

Individual Self Management

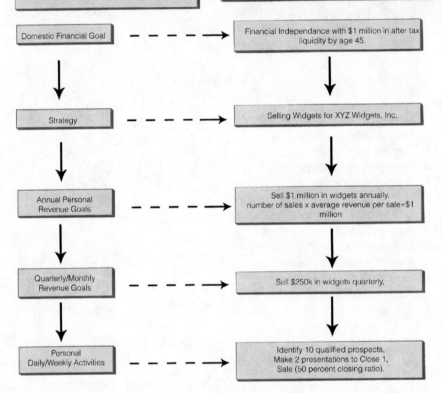

Domestic Mission
To become known in my community as a kind, fair, hardworking, productive member of society and to become a sincere, loving, kind parent and spouse, who displays compassion and understanding to family members, close friends, and neighbors. To conduct all relationships by displaying the qualities of understanding, patience, and tolerance in order to be liked, respected, and admired by the people I meet and know and who know me.

Professional Mission
To become known as the consummate professional seller in my field. To be knowledgeable about my products and services so that I can provide all buyers with a high quality affordable solution to their problems and needs. To be known as a person of the highest ethical standards, who will always be prepared, dependable, punctual, compassionate, and understanding. To be trusted, well liked, and admired by every client and prospect of my company.

Domestic Financial Goal ----→ Financial Independance with $1 million in after tax liquidity by age 45.

Strategy ----→ Selling Widgets for XYZ Widgets, Inc.

Annual Personal Revenue Goals ----→ Sell $1 million in widgets annually, number of sales x average revenue per sale=$1 million

Quarterly/Monthly Revenue Goals ----→ Sell $250k in widgets quarterly,

Personal Daily/Weekly Activities ----→ Identify 10 qualified prospects, Make 2 presentations to Close 1, Sale (50 percent closing ratio).

INDEX

THE AUTHOR

Thirty five years ago, Scott Johnson spent a decade teaching others to sell. In hundreds of intimate classroom settings he counseled aspiring sellers, took notes, and videotaped thousands of role-plays, cataloguing what worked and what didn't.

In the 1980s as vice president of Marketing for an emerging software company, he recruited, hired, trained, and motivated a national sales force. He often accompanied team members on sales calls, taking notes and providing constructive critiques. He then took what he taught and what he learned and applied it to his own real life selling situations, refining as he went; all for the day when he might write this book.

He spent two years gaining product endorsements from boards of directors of state associations of insurance agents and presenting to the top executives of America's largest insurance carriers. It was in this role that Scott refined skills for selling to groups and developed his own system for self-management in order to establish and reach sales related goals.

After teaching thousands of young sellers to sell and manage their time, Scott formed his own speaking and consulting company, JSJ Learning Systems, Inc., and has given time management presentations to associations, businesses, and conventions around the US. Over a period of twenty years, he developed the detailed lessons of this book and the three platforms for a successful career in selling.

Other Works—Scott Johnson first became known for his prose as an editorial writer of the *Agents Confidential* bulletins, published by the Florida Association of Insurance Agents. His weekly exposés and no-holds-barred writing style eventually brought the state bulletins to countrywide recognition. His other works include numerous technical manuals, training guides, and association management texts, including the original guides leading to the Certified Association Executive (CAE) designation—a designation he is one of the youngest Floridians to obtain. Scott was also a charter member of the Accredited Advisor of Insurance designation (AAI), president of the Florida Society of Association Executives, and voted Florida's "Executive of the Year" in 1995.

Scott Johnson's first book reviewed the history of insurance and independent insurance agents and was a milestone in tracing the competitive evolution of the insurance industry away from the cartel mentality toward a more competitive paradigm. F. Lee Bailey's brother and former counsel to the Insurance Information Institute (III) "Bill" Bailey said, "*From Cartels to Competition*...is vintage Scott Johnson—exhaustive research, stimulating and well-choreographed writing, and insightful, often ground-breaking, opinions." *From Cartels to Competition* may be ordered at www.faia.com.

CPSIA information can be obtained at www.ICGtesting.com
Printed in the USA
LVOW072323160911

246637LV00001B/38/P

9 781438 973654